PRAISE FOR *THE DUDE'S GUIDE TO MANHOOD*

"Men need help. They need practical guidance on how to be the men they were created to be. Many men have no map for growing up, loving their wives, fathering their children, and excelling at their jobs. They are doing the best they can, but are falling short. *The Dude's Guide to Manhood* helps men living in the real world access the wisdom they need to live the life they've always wanted."

—RICK WARREN, SADDLEBACK CHURCH

"This book is worth the price for the table of contents. Seriously, God did something quite personal for me before I got any further. But if you try to hand out photocopies of the contents, guys are just going to ask for the rest of it. So buy a bundle, read one, and give the rest to believing and unbelieving guys you know."

—JOHN PIPER, FOUNDER AND TEACHER OF DESIRINGGOD.ORG

"Men want to be strong and successful, respected and revered. But so many walk in defeat and discouragement, living without a plan. If you want to be the man God created you to be, I highly recommend you read *The Dude's Guide to Manhood*."

—CRAIG GROESCHEL, PASTOR OF LIFECHURCH.TV AND AUTHOR OF *FIGHT: WINNING THE BATTLES THAT MATTER MOST*

"I have personally benefited from Darrin Patrick's influence on me both with the Cardinals and at the Journey. What excites me most is that I will get to share the wisdom from this book with my three boys whom I desperately want to be the men that God created them to be."

—MATT HOLLIDAY, SIX-TIME MAJOR LEAGUE BASEBALL ALL-STAR LEFT FIELDER FOR THE ST. LOUIS CARDINALS

"Nothing is more dangerous than a bored man who isn't sure of who he is, what he should be doing, or how he should be doing it. I am encouraged that you have picked this book up. Darrin Patrick leans heavily on the Scriptures as he guides us into a healthy view of manhood. This book doesn't beat you down with all the ways we have failed as men but rather lays out a compelling call to walk in God's good design for us."

—Matt Chandler, lead pastor of teaching at the Village Church and author of *The Explicit Gospel*, *Creature of the Word*, and *To Live Is Christ To Die Is Gain*

"I love Darrin Patrick and I appreciate his masculine expression of Christlikeness. We have tough men and tender men, but hardly any who are truly like Jesus. Let this new resource from Darrin Patrick accelerate your progress in biblical manhood."

—Dr. James MacDonald, senior pastor of Harvest Bible Chapel and author of *Vertical Church* and *Authentic*, jamesmacdonald.com

"Men need to be challenged and equipped. That is exactly what Darrin has done in this short, readable book. I am going to use this book in my own life and in the life of the men I want to influence for Christ."

—Adam Wainwright, MLB all-star and pitcher for the St. Louis Cardinals

"In an age when men are increasingly struggling to live authentic lives, my friend Darrin Patrick has provided a helpful guide to the journey of manhood. Read it with a group of men and challenge one another to live as God intended."

—Ed Stetzer, www.edstetzer.com

"Darrin Patrick is a man of depth and practical precision. He has fought to help men of different ethnicities in his city to be the men that God has called them to be. He has poured out his heart on many occasions wanting to help me want more for God's glory. He spends himself on this passion. Read [this book] and share it with the men in your circle of influence."

—Dr. Eric M. Mason, lead pastor of
Epiphany Fellowship, president of Thriving,
author of *Manhood Restored*

"Mantastic! As manhood erodes around us, it's becoming harder to find real men. The Bible has a lot to say about what it means to be a man—in character and responsibility. This book is an important call for guys to man up and live like real men."

—Ben Peays, executive director, the Gospel Coalition

"Many of us are now physically grown but still have an under-developed understanding of manhood. We need someone who gets how guys think, who can motivate us without guilting us, who can show us a better way. If you are a dude considering this book, my encouragement is simply that you start reading it. I predict you'll have a hard time putting it down. And when you come to the final chapter, you'll want to read the whole thing again."

—Justin Taylor, blogger *Between Two Worlds*;
coauthor of *The Final Days of Jesus*

"Darrin is a dude who's always had a passion for dudes. He has the moral authority to help us rediscover our God-given identity as men!"

—Shawn Lovejoy, direction leader of Mountain Lake
Church and church planters.com; author of *The Measure
of Our Success: An Impassioned Plea to Pastors*

"This book is a must-read for every man out there. We call ourselves men but oftentimes we act like boys. *The Dudes Guide* breaks down what it means to *love* like a man, *train* like a man, and *lead* like a man. It's time to man up, and reading this book is the first step. Let's Freakin Go!"

—SAM ACHO, NFL OUTSIDE LINEBACKER, ARIZONA CARDINALS

The
DUDE'S GUIDE TO
MANHOOD

The
DUDE'S GUIDE TO
MANHOOD

FINDING TRUE MANLINESS IN A
WORLD OF COUNTERFEITS

DARRIN PATRICK

NELSON
BOOKS

An Imprint of Thomas Nelson

Published in Nashville, Tennessee, by Nelson Books, an imprint of Thomas Nelson. Nelson Books and Thomas Nelson are registered trademarks of HarperCollins Christian Publishing, Inc.

Published in association with the literary agency of Wolgemuth & Associates, Inc.

Thomas Nelson titles may be purchased in bulk for educational, business, fundraising, or sales promotional use. For information, please e-mail SpecialMarkets@ThomasNelson.com.

Unless otherwise noted, Scripture quotations are taken from THE NEW KING JAMES VERSION. © 1982 by Thomas Nelson, Inc. Used by permission. All rights reserved.

Scriptures marked NASB are from NEW AMERICAN STANDARD BIBLE®. © The Lockman Foundation 1960, 1962, 1963, 1968, 1971, 1972, 1973, 1975, 1977. Used by permission.

Scripture quotations marked NIV are taken from the Holy Bible, New International Version®, NIV®. Copyright © 1973, 1978, 1984 by Biblica, Inc.™ Used by permission of Zondervan. All rights reserved worldwide. www.zondervan.com

Scriptures marked NLT are from Holy Bible, New Living Translation. © 1996. Used by permission of Tyndale House Publishers, Inc., Wheaton, Illinois 60189. All rights reserved.

Page design by James A. Phinney

Library of Congress Cataloging-in-Publication Data

Patrick, Darrin, 1970-
 The dude's guide to manhood : finding true manliness in a world of counterfeits / Darrin Patrick.
  pages cm
 Includes bibliographical references.
 ISBN 978-1-4002-0547-9
 1. Men (Christian theology) 2. Men--Conduct of life. 3. Christian men--Religious life. I. Title.
 BT703.5.P38 2014
 248.8'42--dc23

                                    2013018753

Printed in the United States of America

15 16 17 RRD 18 17 16 15 14

I dedicate this book to my one and only boy, Drew McKenzie Patrick. Son, you are going to go through many highs and lows in your life. You will fail and you will succeed. You will win and you will lose. I pray that you and I together can learn to be the kind of man I have written about in this book. We both have a good Dad who will never leave us and is faithful to teach us to be the men he created us to be.

CONTENTS

CONTENTS

FOREWORD

BY WILLIE ROBERTSON,
CEO OF DUCK COMMANDER AND
BUCK COMMANDER; EXECUTIVE
PRODUCER OF *DUCK DYNASTY*

YOU GUYS ARE IN FOR A TREAT WITH DARRIN'S BOOK *The Dude's Guide to Manhood*. Nothing draws me to a book more than a big ole manly beard on the cover. I come from a family who not only have mature facial hair but more importantly are mature men who know how to live life and love their wives and kids. It is more crucial than ever for men to rise up to be the men they need to be and impact their friends, families, and their world.

I stand with Darrin in his call for all of us to be better men. It has served me well to surround myself with men who can help me become the man I want to be. So, I have made it my practice to consistently read the Bible as well as other books on leadership and character to help me stay grounded and to excel in what God has called me to do. This is one of those go-to books that will help you become the man you were created to be. It will help you to never lose the desire to be better.

Darrin covered the entire scope of what it means to be a man and offers incredible insight and experience to help us be stronger in all aspects of our manhood—from marriage, to work, to fatherhood, to friendship, and even how we connect with God. It is a man "boot camp" cover to cover.

I have been around, like Darrin, the ultra wealthy, but grew up around the working poor. He and I realize that every man, no matter his socioeconomic status, has the same hopes, dreams, fears, and desires. The famous athlete or high-powered businessman can be just as confused as the shift worker at the local factory.

Money and success do not give us true joy. They may make us happy for a time, but lasting joy comes from something way bigger. Darrin gives answers to the questions we all have as men in a way that lacks being "preachery." His openness about his own life and struggles is a great testament to how God has used him despite his past and weaknesses.

I believe males should really be men. We don't need more boys, we need real men. Strong, godly, mature men. No man is perfect and we will all fall short at times. But this book shows us that we can become stronger and stronger as we allow God to shape us in our weakness. It's sad to say that we even need a *Dude's Guide to Manhood*, but we do. Some of us have lost our way, forgotten who we are and what God wants us to be. I know I was encouraged by reading Darrin's heart put into words and I know you will as well. Oh yeah, and by the way, get to growing those beards out, Boys!!!

FOREWORD

BY STEVEN JACKSON,
NFL RUNNING BACK

WE LIVE IN A WORLD OF BOYS MASQUERADING AS MEN.
It grieves my heart to see our world falling apart mainly
because of the failure of men. As crazy as it might sound, as
men go so goes the world. Men are responsible for much bad,
but they could be responsible for so much good. It is a tragedy
to see so many men living beneath the privilege of true masculinity. Many men want the easy fix, the quick hit, the fast
promotion.

In my career and life I have watched many men fail. They
didn't fail because they weren't passionate. They didn't fail
because they didn't try. They didn't fail because they didn't
work hard. Many of them failed because they didn't prepare
or, more specifically, weren't prepared. They just weren't ready
to be men. Biologically they were ready, able to reproduce.
Vocationally they were ready, empowered by formal or informal
education. But, emotionally and spiritually they were not ready

to assume the responsibilities of manhood. Most of them had no models for how to be men and some of them rejected the models they did have.

What men need is a guide, a coach, someone to help them orient their lives around that which matters the most. Men need to be re-parented and befriended. They need a dad, an older brother. Men need someone to show them the ropes. Men need help.

I have spent my life around the principles of preparation and perseverance. These twin truths are essential functions of being a professional athlete. These are the essential functions of being a man, period. The road we often travel to become "a man" is not one we would ever choose for ourselves. Each of us has our own journey with God that takes us through many peaks and valleys along the way. Figuring out what and how to strengthen, sustain, and endure for the job ahead is the hardest task men face every day.

Darrin Patrick has just made our process and journey that much easier. This book is for men who are trying to be real. This book is for men who are tired of the status quo. This book is for men who want to get better.

Naturally as men we want to figure it all out and know exactly how everything will turn out in the end. However, God has not orchestrated life to be that simple. We need a guide and this book can help men trust God and navigate the path before them with wisdom. From the moment I encountered Darrin Patrick several years ago in a random chapel service, I have found his guidance and intuitiveness to be life changing. I think you will too.

INTRODUCTION

MEN WITHOUT MAPS

I HATE ASKING FOR DIRECTIONS. MOST MEN DO. PART OF
the reason we hate it is that we hate acknowledging that we *don't*
know. We'd like to hide the fact that we have no idea where
we're going. We would rather maintain the illusion that we've
got this. We are grown men, after all, and that means having
everything together and being headed in the right direction.

We pretend to know. We are supposed to know. But we
don't.

Knowing the directions makes the journey more enjoyable.
Life is a lot easier when you know where you need to go. These
days, it's hard to get lost because of the little blue blinking dot
on our GPS app. Our smartphones have delivered us from the
terror of not knowing where we are. They serve as our naviga-
tors for the road, but what we really need is a navigator for life.

Many men are simply unprepared to face the journey of

manhood, in part because they have never been prepared in the first place. Some of us were given maps but never instructed on how to read them. Others were given nothing and were forced to create their own maps. Most of us feel as though we are setting out on a difficult journey without any direction or help. We are on our own, and we don't know where we're going. And it's killing us.

> A MAN WITHOUT A MAP WILL BE A MAN WITHOUT A HEART; HE'LL LACK BOTH PASSION AND COMPASSION.

My own story goes like that. Though my father was around, he was never present. He worked to pay the bills but little else. And I never understood why this was, until we talked one night after he had been drinking.

"When you were about three years old," he told me, "we were all at the dinner table and you were playing around with your food. So I told you to knock it off and eat your damn green beans." My dad slumped in his chair and continued to tell me the story as though it were not about us but about some other father and son. "Your mom and your sisters didn't understand that I was trying to help you become a man. Darrin, men eat what is put before them! I wanted you to be a man and quit playing around at dinner. But every time I tried to coach you, your mom and your sisters started yelling at me, saying I was being too hard on you. I should just leave you alone. So I said, 'Fine, I will leave him the hell alone. *You* raise him.'"

I was stunned. I sat motionless and speechless as I realized the root of my dad's absence in my life, a subject we had never talked about. He had given up on me, left me to myself. My world had caved in on me because, like nearly every toddler in this world, I didn't want to eat my green beans. Because Dad checked out that day, I had to plot my own course on the way to manhood.

The problems in my relationship with my father go beyond the green bean incident, of course. I cannot remember a time when my dad wasn't working. He was good at it, felt affirmed by it, and was addicted to it. It made him come alive. I think it reminded him he was a man—something every man longs to feel.

Needless to say, there wasn't a lot of slacking off in the Patrick household. Dad's mantra was, "If you've got time to lean, then you've got time to clean." I remember as an eight-year-old I would wake up on Sunday mornings jazzed to watch Bryant Gumbel on NBC's *NFL '79*, only to get the call from Dad to go cut firewood. If watching football was like church for me, cutting firewood was communion for Dad.

We didn't go to church, and no one talked about the Bible. My mom wanted me to be a good person, but my dad only wanted me to stay out of trouble.

As I got older, I rejected both my mom's morality and my dad's work ethic. I slept around. I sold drugs so I didn't have to work. I partied. Even the sports I played came easily to me, so I didn't always work hard at that either. I broke the law and took shortcuts to make money, gain friends, and get girls. Later in my life, one of my sisters told me of a conversation with my mother, who had said: "I wouldn't be surprised if Darrin ended up in prison or wound up dead."

After my mom died of cancer, I became more serious about my life and took responsibility for becoming the man I was created to be. Fed up with the emptiness of prolonged adolescence,

I began to reflect more deeply about the man I wanted to become, and I began to pursue mentors and father figures to help me navigate the challenges ahead.

Men tend to run from their fathers. Sometimes this is simply because they are rebels. These sons may have dads who affirm, equip, and empower them for life, but they resist these things to chart their own courses. Some men run because they feel smothered—a dad makes his son into a little god whom he worships and lives vicariously through. Or, as in my case, men run because of abandonment—a dad leaves his son behind physically, emotionally, or spiritually. This trains us to run from potential mentors for fear that they will someday abandon us as well. Dads, through their presence or their absence, define us and the road we will travel.[1]

Many of us are anxious about whether we'll be able to fulfill or escape that definition and rise above the life our fathers showed us. In a poignant scene in the first of the *Lord of the Rings* movies, Aragorn stares at the broken sword of an ancestor who had failed in his duty: "The same blood," he worries, "flows in my veins."[2] It's tempting to think that our biology is our destiny, that our heritage is our future.

These days, though, most men live without a sense of who they are or where they should be going. Their fathers have defined them, but that definition often came through their absence and their lack of instruction. We don't tend to learn a trade from dad anymore. A changing economy has expanded the number of jobs available to men, which has made finding just the right one nearly impossible. It's also harder to find a spouse, as the rituals of dating have been forgotten. And the fathers who know all the contours and valleys of manhood, and who are able and willing to help their sons navigate them, are fewer and farther between. As a result, we are exiled from the company of real men, and we do not know how to return.

It hasn't always been this way. In an older world, rituals and rites of passage would have marked the beginning of manhood for boys. Rituals help a boy relax and rest in his manhood. Manhood was something he entered into—something he earned. Once he had it, no one could take it away. He didn't have to prove himself over and over again. Fathers invented rituals that built a community of men. Dads like this gave their boys a road map to manhood.

A man without a map will be a man without a spine; he'll lack both conviction and courage. A man without a map will be a man without a heart; he'll lack both passion and compassion. And it is those qualities, so essential to true masculinity, that Robin Williams's character, John Keating, tried to help his students discover in the film *Dead Poets Society*.

In the movie, Keating takes his students to the school's trophy rack to view the images of those men who have gone before them. As they look over the photos of the teams of old, the men with their leather football helmets and their missing kneepads, Keating whispers behind them like a ghost: *"Carpe diem.* Seize the day, boys."[3]

> A MAN WITHOUT A MAP WILL BE A MAN WITHOUT A SPINE; HE'LL LACK BOTH CONVICTION AND COURAGE.

The internal voice that haunts men, that whispers to us in the still of the night, may not be saying, "Seize the day." But it secretly reminds us we are not all we could be; we are not the men we were made to be. Men have a strong sense of nostalgia these days, a sense that the true men lived eighty years ago and smoked cigars, had epic beards, and drank scotch. We're trying to fill a gap and overcome the ghost within.

The glory of God revealed through true manhood has been misplaced and forgotten. It's been buried beneath our broken relationships, overworked lives, and persistent and habitual unwillingness to face reality. Men have been left on their own to write their own maps without much help. Is it any wonder that some men overcompensate and become chauvinists or that others shrink back and become cowards?

Our vision for manhood needs help. And the first step in solving the problem is admitting that the problem exists. The second step is realizing that we can't solve it ourselves.

Becoming a man isn't solely based on our efforts. This isn't a self-help manual designed to fix yourself by focusing only on yourself. Manhood, as we'll see, is discovered as we relate to other men.

In the following pages, I aim to provide a guidebook for true manhood. Though I am not a sociologist or psychologist, I am a fellow struggler. I've walked down this road myself, and as a pastor I have helped countless other men do the same. I want to be your coach and navigator through a world that is complex and confusing. In the pages that follow, you will hear stories, be exposed to principles, and learn some drills so that you can be the man you were made to be.

MANY MEN OVERCOMPENSATE FOR A LACK OF FATHERING AND BECOME AGGRESSIVE CHAUVINISTS, WHILE OTHERS SHRINK BACK AND BECOME PASSIVE COWARDS.

ONE

GET IT DONE: BECOME A DETERMINED MAN

DETERMINATION: REFUSING TO QUIT UNTIL WE ACCOMPLISH OUR GOALS

I LOVE WINNING. MY COMPETITIVE FIRE BURNS BRIGHTER than that of most people I know. But I hate losing even more than I love winning. When I approach a game, I am determined to emerge victorious so I don't have to feel that sinking feeling that comes when watching other people celebrate. Competition flows through my veins; it is as natural to me as breathing.

In high school, I was a catcher on our school's baseball team. Even as a sophomore, I emerged as a leader. I was excellent defensively and could hammer almost any fastball thrown at me. My problem was that I couldn't handle Uncle Charley.

Uncle Charley wasn't a coach or a weird relative who inappropriately cheered me on to the point of embarrassment or distraction. Uncle Charley is code for a curveball, and for the life of me I couldn't touch one. I wanted to slam Uncle Charley, but instead I'd weakly pop up every one that came to the plate. Pitchers knew I was setting "dead red" (always looking for a fastball) and began to exploit my weakness. It was worse than isolated moments of failure. I was losing the battle. Pitchers kept me from succeeding by not throwing me fastballs. I was toast, and I hated feeling that weak.

> MEN HIT THE EJECT BUTTON AND HIDE IN JUVENILE BEHAVIOR SUCH AS VIDEO GAMES, PORNOGRAPHY, SPORTS LEAGUES, OR SUBSTANCE ABUSE.

One evening, I was watching a big-league game on television when I heard the famous St. Louis Cardinals broadcaster Jack Buck say, "I've heard that the key to hitting an off-speed pitch is to keep your weight back, keep a good bat path, and try to drive it to the opposite field."[1]

I told my coach and he responded, "Yeah, that's right." And that was all. No offer to help me do the right thing. No encouragement that I could do it. Zero description about how to practice or what mechanics I needed to employ. The not-so-subtle message from this coach (and most men in my life up to that point) was: *You're on your own; go figure it out.*

Frustrated by the lack of guidance, I told one of my teammates about my brief interaction with the coach. My friend told me I needed to work at the tee.

"A tee?! Like, as in T-ball? Like for seven-year-olds?" I asked.

It seemed ridiculous, but I was willing to try anything. If it took devolving into a Little Leaguer to defeat Uncle Charley, then so be it.

So I took a tee into the gym and hit a hundred balls off it every day for two months. My aim was the gap between center and right so that I could hit off-speed pitches to the opposite field (per Jack Buck's advice) in real-game situations. Hitting that curveball never came easy for me, but after the work and repetition, I finally started to experience some success at the plate. Was it ever as easy as hitting a fastball? No. But could I hit it? Yes.

Eventually, I was able to lay off a wicked curveball, drive a decent one to the opposite field, and take a bad one deep. My batting average and homerun totals soared, and I became one of the most feared hitters in my state.

It's amazing how we spend so much of our energy avoiding certain feelings. I poured countless hours into hitting a baseball so I would not feel dominated and controlled by someone else. As is the case for many of us, I didn't pursue transformation until the pain and frustration reached a point where I could not stand them any longer. But when I did finally reach that breaking point, I realized quickly that unyielding determination was indispensable for genuine change.

We can't escape the curveballs and crises in life. What matters is how we prepare ourselves to handle adversities when they come and how we react when they arrive. Some of us are facing serious health problems or family difficulties or are struggling with a loss of hope about our lives. Whatever our situations, whatever is standing in the way, whatever help we fail to receive, a simple question lies before us: are we going to adapt and push through, will we spend the rest of our lives avoiding certain pitches, or will we just quit playing altogether?

Sadly, most men quit. We tend to channel our drive and energy away from overcoming our weaknesses—and toward whatever makes us feel better. Men hit the eject button and hide in juvenile behavior such as video games, pornography, sports leagues, or substance abuse. Other men don't hide in their activities—they hide in themselves. They remain silent, consistently passive, and socially awkward. Still others hide with their friends, delaying marriage or, if married, avoiding connection with their wives.

The effects are the same—many of us avoid real life and escape into a pseudoreality that is more comfortable and less taxing than our own lives. Our wives basically become widows and our children are essentially orphans, left to mourn life alone because the husband and father is no longer present, even though he is at home.

There is a different course, however, which a few discover. When faced with curveballs, some men refuse to allow the challenges before them to prevent them from becoming the men they were created to be. Either they have an innate sense of drive and purpose or their frustrations force them to find one. Rather than mindlessly repeating what isn't working, their determination to succeed drives them toward finding a solution. These men choose to grow, and their resolute commitment to improving their lives means they let no obstacle stand in their way. They become determined men.

The man without determination will always remain one-dimensional. He will remain either a singles hitter or a power hitter with a poor batting average. But he will not be both.

Meeting the challenges before us requires putting in the time to gain the skills we need, skills that broaden and deepen us.

Conversely, the determined man is a growing man. And such growth begins when we honestly confront our limitations and our failures.

TURNING TO FACE THE STRUGGLES OF LIFE

Maybe you are tempted to tap out right now and walk away from the challenge of pursuing the transformation that your employer, family, and friends desperately need. But a more fulfilling, richer, and more adventurous life awaits you. I don't want to see you bail and become another statistic in the decline of manhood in America. I want to challenge you, to call you out so that you live a life of meaning and purpose and glory. Because if you are determined to be alone, you're almost certainly going to fail. All men need to be challenged and called out by others.

You may be thinking, *You just don't understand how hard parts of my life are.* That's precisely the point. Life *is* hard. The world isn't what it should be. People are broken, and we all know it. Becoming a determined man doesn't mean you have to ignore pain. It means replacing casual effort with supernatural strength to persevere in the midst of uncomfortable circumstances. Determination isn't

DETERMINATION ISN'T ALWAYS ABOUT SUCCEEDING. SOMETIMES DETERMINATION SIMPLY MEANS SURVIVING, PRESSING ON IN THE FACE OF WHAT FEELS LIKE INSURMOUNTABLE OBSTACLES.

always about succeeding. Sometimes determination means simply surviving, pressing on in the face of what feels like insurmountable obstacles. But as men, we need to realize that our friends and families depend on us to become all we are called to be.

DRILL: List your top three goals in life. Make them specific. Identify the step you can accomplish in the next twenty-four hours and commit to doing it.

Remember the story my dad told me about the green beans? He had a choice to access supernatural strength in dealing with me. Though my sisters and mother made it difficult for him to lead well, he could have adjusted. He could have engaged me personally and attempted to train me in my eating habits. Instead, he ignored me. My existence, even when he tried to ignore it, reminded him of his lack of resources and doubtlessly aroused feelings of powerlessness and uncertainty. Dad had an opportunity to jump in the deep end of the parenting pool, but he played it safe and chose to splash around in the shallows.

My father did the best with what he had. He parented as he had been parented.[2] The more I realize that, the easier it is to forgive him. But when he was told that what he was doing wasn't working, he didn't spend time working on the tee to figure it out. He quit. I love my dad dearly, but I desperately wish he had had the courage and determination to persevere in what did not come easily for him.

My own sense of determination was hindered by my dad's failure to model it for me, and by his unwillingness to call me to live by a deeper standard than simply pursuing what I wanted at the moment. Even if I had the inner drive to succeed, I didn't know which direction I should go. And so I eventually found surrogate fathers who helped me navigate the challenges I faced. I needed them; determination isn't something that most of us can cultivate on our own.

Think about it. What is stopping you? What is keeping you from living up to your God-given potential? Where have you quit? Are you doing anything that those who are close to you wish you would not do? Every man needs to consider the cost of failing to persevere in overcoming the difficulties he faces. Just as off-speed pitches dominated me, suffering or the mundane rhythms of everyday life may be dominating you. The people who care about you are waiting for you to spend some time on the tee and get back in the batter's box and take a swing.

LOSE YOUR EXCUSES

My friend James grew up in the hood, on a street where drugs were sold directly outside his house and people had gunfights in broad daylight. His dad was the most popular guy in the neighborhood because he could fix anything. He changed neighbors' oil, patched their roofs, and adjusted their transmissions—and all people had to do was ask. His dad was famous for working hard, being the life of the party, and helping anyone. But his dad was also famous for selling drugs to teenagers and being a player with the ladies.

As dangerous as it was outside James's house, it might have been more dangerous inside the house. James's dad was physically abusive. On several occasions, James broke up physical altercations between his mom and dad, which on one occasion ended with his dad shoving his wife's head through the sheetrock. The situation only grew more desperate when James's dad began shacking up with another woman. The infidelity crushed James, not only because of how it disrespected his mom, himself, and his siblings, but also because of the embarrassment he felt from his neighbors. The woman his dad shacked up with lived in the same neighborhood.

For years, James used his upbringing as an excuse for a lack of focus, direction, and drive to maximize his talents. Eventually, however, he realized that his past did not have to determine his life and that he could transform the tombstone of his history into a monument to God's grace. James now owns a thriving business, and he has overcome the shame of the way he grew up.

Nike got things half right. Eventually, we need to "Just Do It." At the heart of determination is a resolute decision to do something and to not stop until it is done. But our energy and effort are spoiled unless we do the right thing. To determine is simply to say no to one thing and yes to something else. In developing determination, we must face the past and discern both the right path forward and those obstacles that will hinder us as we walk down that path. The choices may not be easy, nor may they be safe, but we cannot escape them.

The world is littered with stories like James's. Most men don't make it out of tough neighborhoods or rough upbringings. The few who do rise up don't allow others' choices to define their lives. They lose their excuses and quit viewing themselves as victims of their circumstances.

CONVINCE YOUR HEAD, AND YOUR BODY WILL FOLLOW

There are few people who embody determination like Tiger Woods. Most of us were not set on a path toward athletic dominance before age two, but Tiger was. His father had a vision—Tiger would beat all of golf's records, including Jack Nicklaus's hallowed eighteen major championships. Most golfers rarely shoot nine holes under 50 strokes, but Tiger did it at age three! He broke 80 for a full round at age eight. Then he broke 70 at age twelve. By the time he went pro in 1996, he had won every major amateur championship there was, and most of them more than once. He won the Junior Amateur title three straight years and then won the Amateur title the next three years, at the same time winning his high school and Division I college championships. Six months after turning pro, he won the Masters by 12 strokes. From 1999 to 2002, he broke nearly every major championship record and was the first player to hold all four major championships at once.

Research by university statisticians actually showed that other golfers played worse when Tiger was on the course.[3] The stats show they actually did not try as hard because they knew they were playing for second place. That's dominance.

Despite Tiger's struggles on and off the golf course, his mythological status as the most intimidating figure in golf remained.

9

Even while his life was falling apart, few people doubted that he would eventually return to the top levels of golf, even if he would never be the automatic, dominant player he once was.

DRILL: Identify a place in your life where you feel your thoughts are out of control. Call a friend and let him know your discouragement and ask for regular phone conversations to talk through the roadblock.

Yet the problems Tiger needed to overcome to return to his peak form weren't just with his hands; they were also between his ears. That was the assessment, at least, of Jack Nicklaus. When asked about Tiger's game, he said, "I don't know what goes [on] between his ears. That's really the X factor. His golf game and his golf swing look pretty similar to what I've been looking at and he hits a lot of great shots. But you never know what's going on in somebody's head."[4]

Some of us are beaten before we even play. We don't expect to win. Half the battle is in having the determination that no matter what stands in our way, we will not quit. We may not win the game, get the promotion, or save the marriage, but it won't be because of a lack of determination or effort.

STAY IN THE PRESENT

One of the hardest things for most guys is the temptation to live in the past, or what I like to call the Uncle Rico Syndrome. Remember him from the quirky film *Napoleon Dynamite*? Rico was Napoleon's uncle who always talked about what he could have done: "Oh, man, I wish I could go back in time. I'd take state." Watching Rico is amusing, but it also hits painfully close to home for some of us.

This was the case for my friend Skip, who excelled in the performing arts in high school. He dreamed of performing on Broadway and winning Tony awards. But instead of moving to New York, he went to college in the Midwest. He bounced around doing community theater, usually becoming the star of the show.

Fast-forward twenty years: Skip can quote almost any song lyric from any current Broadway show by memory. Being in New York and on Broadway is constantly on his mind. He is nearly forty, and he still talks about how he wishes he had chosen a different course decades ago. His Facebook updates reveal the pain he suffers from his unrealized potential.

> DETERMINED MEN REFUSE THE NOSTALGIA OF THE PAST OR THE SPECULATION OF THE FUTURE. INSTEAD, THEY EMBRACE THE PRESENT.

Other guys don't live in the past; they dream about the future, which can be equally damaging. They dream about that lake house, better vacations, or an evening with a particular lady. Our daydreams reveal a lot: *Things may be hard now. It might be painful or boring. But just wait. One day . . .* Many of us are going to do great things when we graduate, when we get married, when we get promoted, when we get our dream homes, or when we get in shape.

But what about *now*? Determined men refuse the nostalgia of the past or the speculation of the future. Instead, they embrace the present because they know that every choice right now determines how the future will look. They don't shrink from reality but courageously confront it. They stare down the temptation to escape into the past or daydream about the days ahead, while fighting to embrace the world around them even as they seek to change it for the better.

REHABILITATE THE BROKEN

For years I have had chronic back pain. Even as I sit and write, I am reminded that I must get up at least four times an hour or feel the consequences. Over the years I have been to dozens of chiropractors, physical therapists, and surgeons who have offered counsel and, in many cases, tried to cure me. Recently, I found help in the form of a multidisciplined doctor who has a holistic view and solutions for dudes with bad backs.

My first meeting with this doctor was both wonderful and terrible. It was awesome to have someone who really understood my lifestyle as a man and also was astute at identifying the sources of my misery. He treated me with a newer technique called active release therapy, which resulted in immediate relief. As I was benefiting from his magical hands, I was flooded with hope that I might not have to spend the rest of my life in pain. After the treatment the good doctor stepped out of the room and said he would return shortly with my treatment plan. Based on previous experience, I figured I would be seeing him once a week for treatment and that would be the path to healing.

When he returned, my hope left the room as he discussed

my *two-year* process to health. There was a weekly treatment involved, as I suspected, but also a nuanced nutrition plan replete with dietary restrictions and supplements. There was also daily homework. This would be no easy path if I wanted real healing.

Over the years, I have had the privilege of working with several active and retired professional athletes. To be a professional athlete means a life of rehab. Athletes must focus on training the weak areas of the body in order to deal with nagging injuries. It is really easy, they say, to major on their strengths and avoid their weaknesses. Many athletes overtrain in one area and neglect other areas, which is why many of them are often injured.

WILL YOU LEAD YOUR LIFE, OR WILL YOU LET IT LEAD YOU?

We can take instruction in the physical realm and apply it to the spiritual: "Confront your weakness, give focused attention to it, and do rehab till you are healthy."

Our difficult duty is to recognize that these "nagging injuries" are also opportunities to develop the determination we need to become the men God has made us to be.

BUY TIME

I was listening to a pastor named Wayne Barber when he quoted a strange verse from the Bible that talked about purchasing time. He then asked an interesting question: "How do you purchase time?"[5] I could not think of an answer. Thankfully, he answered his own question: "You buy time with the choices you make." He was unpacking the ancient Greek word *exagorazo* that may be best captured by our current word *redeem*.

The word *redeem* was used in common business in the ancient Greco-Roman world. To redeem was to capitalize on the market by wise investment. You "redeemed" your money when your returns dwarfed your original investment. You can redeem time, as you can money, by making the most of the time you have with good choices.

Determined men realize that they have twenty-four hours in a day, and if they waste time it is because they intend to do so. Determined men take time seriously and are very intentional about how they use it. This does not mean we never rest—far from it! But it does mean we should be intentional about when and how we rest.

For most of us, redeeming time probably does not mean spending hours each night watching television, surfing YouTube, or dinking around in the garage. Such activities may feel relaxing in the moment, but they are often a drain on our energy and ability to uphold our many responsibilities. For most of us, redeeming time will mean that we work hard to eliminate unnecessary time suckers in our week, design systems for answering e-mails efficiently, think through our weekly schedules and priorities beforehand, and live by predetermined goals.

LIFE IS PURSUING YOU, AND IT WILL FIND YOU OUT.

Your life is before you. The adventure and challenge you long for will not be satisfied by vicariously living through your sports teams. The meaning and the purpose you have been made for will not be discovered on the couch. Life is pursuing you, and it will find you out. You can try to avoid the curveballs, drowning out the challenges and obstacles of life with hobbies and TV. But at some point a crisis will arise, and you will be faced with a decision to press on or check out. What will you choose to do the moment it arrives? Will you lead your life, or will you let it lead you?

TWO

PAY ATTENTION AND LEARN SOMETHING: BECOME A COACHABLE MAN

COACHABLE: SOMEONE WHO IS WILLING TO TAKE AND RESPOND RIGHTLY TO CRITIQUE

WILL HUNTING IS ADRIFT. AN UNMOTIVATED GENIUS, Will works blue-collar jobs between stints in jail. Rather than joining the ranks of the students, he works as a janitor for the prestigious university MIT. Abused as a child, Hunting buries his massive potential under a hazy cloud of rebellion and apathy. He is only discovered after solving complex math problems on hallway blackboards after hours.[1]

Even though he's brilliant, Will Hunting needs to be coached. The help he needs comes in the form of two very different mentors.

Professor Gerald Lambeau agrees to guide his academic work and tutor him so he can succeed professionally. And Sean Maguire, a rebellious and unorthodox counselor who had been Lambeau's former classmate, becomes Hunting's therapist.

Will's life is marked by the contrast between the two coaches. Lambeau, a seemingly perfect man, is initially intrigued by Will's ability but eventually becomes threatened by it. As many of us have experienced from mentors, Lambeau appears to be for Will, but is actually for himself. Hunting's therapist, Sean Maguire, is the opposite of Lambeau. Though he is an accomplished psychologist with brilliant insight into others, he doesn't have his life together and doesn't pretend to. Sean leaves a lot wanting in his own character, but he doesn't want anything from Will. Maguire's challenge is simple for the young genius: acknowledge his wounds and be willing to learn, or remain uncoachable and live beneath his masculine privilege.

WE DON'T WAKE UP AS MEN ONE DAY, AND WE DON'T STUMBLE INTO IT.

Great coaches see something in us that we can't see ourselves, and they work patiently with us to call it out of us. A great coach helps us become who we are and discover the buried inner glory that is waiting to emerge.

But great coaches also challenge us to see something new in the world. They expand our horizons and introduce us to areas that we never knew existed. They raise our gaze beyond ourselves toward the physical and spiritual worlds. They open our eyes so that new things don't threaten us, because we have the courage to embrace, grow, and learn.

True manhood isn't unearthed by accident. It doesn't simply happen as we get older or as our circumstances change. We don't wake up as men one day, and we don't stumble into it. It is handed down from one generation to the next. It is passed on from those who have learned from others to those who are on the outside looking in. Only the coachable can walk the long path into true manhood.

Will Hunting's choice is one we must all face.

WHO WILL TEACH MEN TO BE MEN?

"It seems like everyone around here wants you to be their dad." That's what my friend Jeremy observed about many of the young leaders in one of the organizations I lead. He had only been on our staff a few weeks when I asked him his impressions, and he didn't hold back. He's a straightforward guy who doesn't pull his punches. "This is a needy bunch of dudes," he said.

Jeremy can spot neediness largely because he isn't needy. He has no animosity, no bitterness, no sense of disappointment or entitlement about his upbringing. His dad coached his sports teams without being "that dad." They rebuilt a car together, working in the afternoons in their garage. His dad cooked him breakfast many mornings before school. They spent a lot of time together and Jeremy was mentored well.

There is nothing a young man wants more than for his dad to be a good coach, to bring him into the company of men and introduce him to its mysteries, challenges, and opportunities. He wants his father not only to know the sort of technical things guys are supposed to know but also to be the sort of person he can imitate. He wants a dad who is stable, secure, hopeful, tough, and tender.

A man's glory emerges when his father draws it out of him and affirms it despite those who can't yet see it. A good man is a good teacher. He sees in his son more potential than the son can see himself and helps his son enter into the fullness of manhood.

But there aren't many Jeremys in this world, nor many fathers like his. Most men never have their masculine glory unearthed for them; it's still buried, forgotten, and neglected.

Think about *Knocked Up*, a film by contemporary king of comedy Judd Apatow that portrays the rampant apathy of many younger men. Ben, a pathetic kid who is trying to start a pornography website, impregnates an attractive, career-driven woman and is forced to confront his own incompetence. In a telling conversation with his father, Ben acknowledges, "I don't know how to take responsibility for myself . . . I don't know what to do. I'm an idiot. Tell me what to do!"[2] His father is similarly clueless; he can only stammer that he has no idea, but he loves Ben.

Within every man there is the potential for true manhood. If they learn how to, men can exercise self-control and leadership in any and every situation. But without fathers to help us discover that in healthy ways, we can end up never cultivating our manhood or abusing it and others around us.

COVERING UP THE FELT ABSENCE

At some point, we've all felt that we are cosmically insignificant—and then we work to bury that feeling as deep as we can. We know we really are not the unique snowflakes our elementary teachers said we were. We have an inward sense that there is little substance to us. We are shallow and empty, regardless of how firm and tough the outside looks. And we know it.

Yet we don't want anyone else to know how empty we are, and so we keep the truth about ourselves buried—which includes destroying our willingness to be taught. Perhaps the word *conceit* best describes this hiding of our emptiness. Most of the time *conceited* reminds us of people who think they are better than others. But really, a conceited man is desperately trying to prove to himself that he is indeed something.

Men consumed with filling their own emptiness rather than acknowledging it cannot be taught. If we spend our time and energy posing and posturing, we'll only hear the criticism and not the constructiveness. Instead of craving help, we reject it because it feels like a threat to our manhood. The very thing we need most to enter into true manhood is the very thing we can't stand.

> AT SOME POINT, WE'VE ALL FELT THAT WE ARE COSMICALLY INSIGNIFICANT—AND THEN WE WORK TO BURY THAT FEELING AS DEEP AS WE CAN.

The ancient Greeks had an interesting word that captures the plight of many men: *kenodoxia*, the combination of *kenós* and *doxa*. To say something had "doxa" was to say it had meaning, glory, and importance. There is a weightiness to it, a sense of gravity. *Kenós* simply means "empty." *Kenodoxia* means "empty of glory."[3]

Things that are empty of glory have no substance, depth, or power. Just like the idiom "it doesn't matter" suggests, things that are empty of glory aren't worth talking about. The word *kenodoxia* is getting at the same sort of thing, except at a deeper level. Christian theologians often talk about how humans live in a world that is broken because of sin. The world doesn't work the way it is supposed to, and neither do we. *Kenodoxia* describes the destructive effect of sin and brokenness on the soul of a man.

Learning to be coachable is impossible for men who are attempting to cover up their own lack of glory. Some men want to maintain the illusion of control, so they never acknowledge their ignorance. Others want to come up with all the ideas so they don't have to share the glory with anyone. Others don't want to do the work of pursuing transformation and growth because they think they've already arrived. And some don't want to ask for help because they know the culture disapproves of men looking "weak" and they want, more than anything, the approval of those around them.

We have learned to fake it well. But deep down within us, we all really want to be taught.

BECOMING COACHABLE MEN

If we're going to become coachable men, we have to do away with our excuses and confront our lives head-on. We can learn to be coachable. We don't have to pretend we have all the answers or that we don't need any help. But to do that, we have to change our lives in ways that will be uncomfortable and quit making excuses.

Your History as an Excuse

You grew up in a dysfunctional family. Period. For many of you, there is no argument about that. You either didn't have a father or, like James, had a father who obviously hurt you. For others, like Jeremy, there might be some disagreement. But even he would admit that his family wasn't perfect and that on some level there was a gap between what was and what ought to have been. No matter how great our dads were, they sometimes came up short. Your dad probably did the best he could with the tools he had, but he didn't have all the right tools and didn't always use the proper tool at the proper time.

You need a new dad. I am not saying you have to discard the old man or purge from your memory the good things he has passed on. We need to reconcile with our fathers and open ourselves to learning from them. But some of you might also need new, older mentors who can help father you as you continue to grow into manhood.

> YOUR DAD PROBABLY DID THE BEST HE COULD WITH THE TOOLS HE HAD, BUT HE DIDN'T HAVE ALL THE RIGHT TOOLS AND DIDN'T ALWAYS USE THE PROPER TOOL AT THE PROPER TIME.

We also need to quit using our fathers as excuses for our lives now. It is too easy to blame everything on our "dad issues." They're important, yes, but once we recognize them, we have to begin to take responsibility for ourselves and accept our own roles in our problems. Many men are tempted to look at others for their problems when they should be looking at themselves.

Success as an Excuse

We have tricked ourselves into believing we don't need coaches just because we've grown up without them. "After all, I made it this far without them," we tell ourselves. But being teachable means facing our weaknesses and our ignorance and having the courage and humility to change. A little success can get in the way of leading the sort of life we've been made for. It's easy to get comfortable, to justify ourselves, and to act as if we're okay simply because we have good jobs and good-looking families. But if we are going to be coachable and grow, we need to be grateful for our successes without clinging to them.

How can men become coachable, then?

Dig up the desire for it or the circumstances will force it on us. At some point, every man reaches his limits in one part of his life. We all discover a curveball that we just cannot hit. Whether it's money, family, marriage, work, or our emotional life, none of us knows everything on our own. But if we cultivate the desire to learn and grow before we reach those limits, then we won't be threatened by them or run from them.

Cultivate relationships with others before we need them. The best way to grow before our circumstances force us to is to cultivate relationships with others. There is no coachability apart from the risk and accountability that comes with being in relationships with others. We have been hurt in relationships, but we are also healed in relationships. Coachable men know they can't get true wisdom regarding relationships with the opposite sex from the Internet or *Maxim*. They seek out a true man who has navigated such waters before. Men can learn to install a flat screen from a YouTube video, but we can only learn the essence of manhood by being welcomed into the fraternity by another member.

Humble ourselves and ask for guidance. Asking for help is hard for men. We come up with a thousand reasons why we shouldn't. We tell ourselves that others aren't interested in helping us, or that we'll burden them too much. Or we tell ourselves that we don't need help, that we're doing okay. There is no escaping it: asking for guidance takes humility, and humility will only begin in us when we confront our own fundamental *kenodoxia,* our own lack of inner glory. When we recognize that, we will see we need help and begin to recognize as well how eager other men are to help us.

Find a team of mentors. No one has just one perfect mentor. Everyone is looking for the elusive guy who can teach us everything we need to know. But it is very unlikely that you will find one man who can father you in all the areas of your life. You should probably stop looking for one new dad and instead look for several.

There are a host of mentors all around us. No one is perfect, but the teachable man can learn from anyone. Cultivating a coachable heart means learning to recognize the best qualities of others and then imitating them. Children, the mentally challenged, and even our family members and biological brothers can be helpful mentors if we have eyes to see and ears to hear.

> DRILL: Who are the men you have met that you respect most? Send them an e-mail or call them right now to set up coffee; then list ten questions you want to ask them.

I have a "dad" who helps me with prayer. It's hard for me to admit, but I really struggle to pray. I am a doer, not a sitter. But I need to learn how to be silent, how to embrace solitude, and how to talk to God. So one of my dads helps me. I have a dad who is good with money. My biological dad once told me that his philosophy of money was that if he had checks, then he assumed he had money. He was kidding, kind of. But he wasn't great with finances, so I found a financial dad. I needed a dad who knew how to manage a complex organization, so I found a retired businessman who had been very successful. He agreed to come alongside and mentor me, teaching me how to manage myself and my organization.

THE FIRST STEP TOWARD TEACHABILITY IS RECOGNIZING THAT WE HAVE EVERYTHING TO LEARN AND WE CAN LEARN PARTS OF IT FROM SEVERAL PEOPLE.

Waiting for the perfect mentor can be a sign of pride. It reveals that we think we are so good that we can only learn from the greatest. But the first step toward teachability is recognizing that we have everything to learn and we can learn parts of it from several people.

THE ONGOING GOOD OF BEING COACHABLE

The man who refuses to grow is dying a slow death. Learning is like oxygen in our lungs or cold water on a hot day. It's what we are made for. Being taught unearths our core, and it helps us discover that at the center is a learner who can also teach—a person who both receives and gives.

Learning is at the heart of being a man. Those who refuse to learn, who close off themselves from growth, cut themselves off from their own manhood. It is easy to remain ignorant. It is easy to fear change. Learning takes a lot of time and challenges our assumptions. Confronting our own ignorance and need disorients us, disrupts us, and moves us out of our comfort zones. But it also invites us into a bigger life—the life we've always wanted.

THREE

TRAIN, DON'T JUST TRY: BECOME A DISCIPLINED MAN

DISCIPLINE: DOING WHAT YOU DON'T WANT TO DO SO YOU'RE FREE TO DO WHAT YOU DO WANT TO DO

REMEMBER 9/11 AND THE IMAGES OF BURNING BUILDINGS and people jumping to their deaths? It was a new kind of horror for America, a new sort of warfare. Like all tragedies, the pain of the victims that day was unspeakable. But suffering often produces heroes as well as victims, and there were many heroes that day.

Among them was Rick Rescorla, who kept twenty-seven hundred team members of the Morgan Stanley investment firm safe by helping them calmly exit the World Trade Center.

He was a model of leadership, barking out clear orders on his megaphone to keep people moving efficiently. He sang fighting songs he had learned as a boy in England to keep people cheerful. And at the end of it, he gave even his life; he was in the tower when it fell, making one final sweep to ensure that everyone else had made it out alive.

The remarkable tale of Rick Rescorla begins long before that horrible day, though. After a truck loaded with explosives detonated in the World Trade Center's garage in 1993, Rescorla realized that the only other point at which the building was vulnerable was by air. He mused about what might happen if a plane loaded with explosives was flown into the building, and even tried unsuccessfully to persuade Morgan Stanley to move their offices across the Hudson River to New Jersey.

Convinced that an attack would come someday, Rescorla had the entire Morgan Stanley staff rehearse their evacuation plan every three months. As a former soldier, Rescorla understood the importance of drills, of practice making perfect. A friend even described him as "fanatical" about practicing evacuations. But when the crisis eventually came, people were prepared.[1]

Rescorla didn't simply try to save people in the middle of a crisis; he trained in such a way that he was able to. He understood a disappearing value for many men: discipline. Discipline is rarely enjoyable, but almost always profitable. Cultivating a disciplined life means doing what we don't want to do to give ourselves the freedom to do what we need to do.[2] Yet as H. L. Mencken said, "The average man doesn't want to be free. He wants to be safe."[3] Which is partly why most of us don't want to change. It's too uncomfortable and too difficult, and our current habits seem to work well enough.

Everyone has habits that help accomplish his goals with relative ease. Most people have enough sense to work hard in one area of their lives (school, work, relationships, hobbies) so they can excel. The question is not so much whether we have discipline or not. The question is whether our disciplines and habits are leading us toward true manhood.

We may have some discipline, in other words, but we often limit its scope. It is easy to quarantine our habits to one part of our lives, allowing other parts to remain untouched. We often look at great athletes as models of professional discipline, even though many are total failures at personal discipline. Michael Jordan may have been the best basketball player ever, and he was certainly one of the hardest workers at it. Yet he has (so far) failed as a front-office guy and as an owner. Tiger Woods might be the most talented golfer on the planet, but he couldn't keep his pants on and be faithful to his supermodel wife.

It is easy to be judgmental of entertainers and athletes as we observe their personal lives spinning out of control. It's much harder to see how those same dynamics are at work in less extreme ways in our own hearts. But if we avoid cultivating discipline in every part of our lives, we leave our manhood buried and set ourselves up for failure.

THE PORNIFICATION OF LIFE AND THE PURSUIT OF DISCIPLINE

Sociologist Pamela Paul has taken to calling our society "pornified."[4] Our view of sex and people has been so shaped by pornography that everything now has to titillate us to get our attention. Want to sell hamburgers? Use a surgically enhanced woman wearing Daisy Dukes while washing a car. It doesn't matter that the two are totally disconnected. In a pornified society, cheap and easy thrills are the key to seducing the masculine heart.

Pornification extends well beyond sex, though. At the heart of pornography is a pursuit of a short-term pleasure at the expense of a long-term good. Porn is a quick fix that doesn't fix anything. It gives us an intense experience without any effort or any risk. It's a sugar high that leaves us starving.

A pornified society focuses on the experiences we want to have rather than the people we need to become.[5] We are a society of experience chasers—especially men. Just ponder the contents of our bucket lists, which is a litmus test for how pornified we are. Many of our lists contain skydiving. Why? It's conquering a fear; it's risky. It is the Rolls-Royce of adrenaline highs. Jumping out of a plane says to the world, "I refuse to be a boring person," and says to ourselves, "Maybe this will shake me out of my boring life." In one experience we have something to justify our own existence and a great story to tell at parties.

PORN IS A QUICK FIX THAT DOESN'T FIX ANYTHING.

Skydiving gives us the momentary impression that we're alive. But once the adrenaline high goes away, we are left to seek yet another new experience rather than develop better character. Just as men who watch porn perpetually seek more intense thrills, so experience chasers must move from thrill to thrill in order to keep the experiences intense. Pornification is alive and well, while discipline and determination are wasting away.[6]

Think about the young, single, upwardly mobile man who lives for food, women, and must-see sporting events. Or the midlife crisis guy who trades in his wife of twenty-five years for a twenty-five-year-old, buys a sports car, and gets a face-lift. It isn't the desire for excitement that is the problem, but it's the lack of delight-inspiring discipline that dries up the souls of such pleasure-addicted men.

We need better men, who work hard, play well, and age gracefully. What if our weekends weren't all about us? What if we could channel some of our risk-taking, experience-grabbing passion into the cultivation of character? What if we had a generation of guys, each growing old with the wife of his youth instead of taking a new, youthful wife? What if we quit investing in toys and invested in a legacy that endures?

Discipline trains us in the art of focusing on our real needs instead of being obsessed with our felt needs. To be disciplined is to learn to say no to the quick fix in lieu of the better reward. Take my friend Joe, for example. He could have continued his career well into his midfifties, which would have grown his already escalating personal wealth. Instead he chose to help younger businessmen start and excel in their careers by giving valuable capital and even more valuable mentoring.

> DRILL: Nearly every guy needs to change the way he eats. Take some time and list the past ten full meals you've eaten. Did you (a) eat badly or (b) eat too much? Ask your wife to help you create a new diet and find rewards for sticking with it.

Disciplined men still enjoy their lives. But they do so in ways that build their character and extend their legacies. Men who enjoy their lives in a disciplined way change the world because they aren't ruled by it.

Disciplined men aren't simply men who have to win and are overfueled with adrenaline. Such men realize that a life where the highs aren't quite as high and the lows aren't quite as low has its own rewards. They are steady, but the permanent and lifelong goods they seek make life truly an adventure. Rather than continuing in the boring repetition of the pleasures of prolonged adolescence, true men keep their eyes fixed on a better reward and the goods of a more permanent legacy.

WE NEED BETTER MEN, WHO WORK HARD, PLAY WELL, AND AGE GRACEFULLY.

THE END OF SHORTCUTS

As I mentioned earlier, I grew up playing sports. I was always active. That was a habit that made the choice of not watching television an easy one for me. Ask me whether I was disciplined, and I would never have known it. Grazing on fruit and protein throughout the day rather than eating two big meals and snacking on foods that ended with "-itos" was a discipline I had, but I didn't realize it. The disciplines of going to practice and lifting weights were built into my routine, but by other people.

I didn't have a problem with weight gain until after college. Until that point I had engaged in athletics, so my weight-training routine was set for me. But when I left organized sports behind, the fat began to gather on *my* behind. When that happens to a man, it's easy to blame a slowing metabolism or, if you're a frat fellow, the binge drinking. But the reason I was fit before wasn't related to my biochemistry.

Beginning just after college, I tried to get back in shape. I started with basketball, but that was an anaerobic sport and didn't do much other than get me hurt or into fights. I tried the Atkins diet, but that was too radical, so I moved to the South Beach diet. I was so desperate, I handed in my man card and went to step aerobics with my wife. I began to watch infomercials and was even convinced by Suzanne Somers to purchase an Ab Dolly.

But it wasn't until recently that I began disciplining myself about what sort of foods I eat, built a more realistic assessment of myself, and came under the supervision of a physical therapist and a professional trainer. And I have made genuine progress.

The biggest obstacle to men gaining discipline is the fact that they have tried it before.

Like my early attempts at losing weight, we jump from quick fix to quick fix to get results with as little effort as possible. *Trying* is a short-term attempt to see if something works. "Sure, I'll try that," we say. And we have had plenty of trying. We have tried to get in shape, tried to connect with our wives, tried to get better jobs, tried to be more spiritual. We have tried and are tired from it.

Accomplishing anything of significance doesn't happen because we *try* really hard but because we *train* really well. We can try a new restaurant or try a different wardrobe. We can even try a better diet. But we can't just try to get our waistlines back to high school proportions. We can't just try to bench-press three hundred pounds. One author put it this way: discipline is "any activity I can do by direct effort that will help me do what I cannot now do by direct effort."[7] By direct effort most of us cannot just go run a marathon right now. But give us twelve months of training and we might have a shot. By direct effort we can't simply lose twenty pounds. But if we train our bodies by working out and train our appetites to love healthy food, the fat will melt away and stay off.

> Discipline is "any activity I can do by direct effort that will help me do what I cannot now do by direct effort."
> —John Ortberg

DRILL: Exercise. Literally. Pull out your calendar. Look through the past month and identify the number of times you worked out your body in a strenuous way, whether at work or through playing in a gym league or something like that, or by walking intentionally if you are no longer able to do strenuous activity. Go work up a sweat right now and reflect about how good it feels.

It's tempting to always look for shortcuts, to go for the maximum results with the least amount of effort. And we have been sold a version of change that says we can, provided we purchase the necessary pharmaceuticals. For a muscular body and rippling abs, pop some supplements and steroids. Want sexual excitement when you're old without needing the intimacy to really bring it? There's a magic blue pill for you. Most of us are probably never going to be the "Most Interesting Man in the World." But we can drink a certain Mexican beverage and feel for a moment as though we are. Many of the diets we try and most of the workout equipment we buy are fads, sold to us on the promise that we can find a shortcut to happiness.

But that's not the way things normally work. We have to pay the price at first and learn discipline, at least if we want to keep the goods around long at all. No student goes into a test and says, "I want to make this as hard as I can on myself." If the goal isn't merely passing the test but gaining the wisdom from the material, we will approach the test with a seriousness and intentionality that we wouldn't have otherwise. We will become more efficient in our studies without shortchanging the process and undermining the desired outcome of our learning.

Discipline was never meant to be quarantined to one or two areas of life. It is designed to bleed out into every area. If that's your goal, there are no shortcuts. If you do not let discipline have full sway over your entire life, you are stunting yourself, keeping yourself from being the sort of man you were created to be, and hindering your joy.

THE DISCIPLINES OF FREEDOM

Discipline is for freedom. The person who practices an instrument doesn't simply practice for practice's sake. The goal is to have the freedom to play, the ability to sit down and successfully press the keys he wants to press on a piano or pluck the strings on a guitar in a way that makes beautiful music. Discipline temporarily constrains and constricts us for the purpose of making available a greater good. When we are disciplined, we say no to more immediate pleasures, but yes to long-term fulfillment. Discipline limits us for a season in order to deepen our ability to enjoy the world and develop the character and skills within us that we need to flourish.

Consider what Theodore Roosevelt, who is sometimes regarded as a "man's man," said:

> In this life we get nothing save by effort. Freedom from effort in the present merely means that there has been stored up effort in the past. A man can be freed from the necessity of work only by the fact that he or his fathers before him have worked to good purpose. . . . A mere life of ease is not in the end a very satisfactory life, and, above all, it is a life which ultimately unfits those who follow it for serious work in the world.[8]

Our lack of discipline destroys our freedom. Because we try and don't train wisely, we end up being emotionally driven. We are slaves to the spectacular and the spontaneous. Most men would rather be entertained than be a part of transforming the world, and that erodes manliness and undercuts our confidence. If we can't control ourselves, then we will be controlled by everything else. The angry, domineering masculinity that is so dangerous arises in part because impotent men lack self-control. They lash out because they are frustrated that they cannot control others around them. But they do not control themselves, either, and self-control is where true freedom begins.

THE DEADLY PURSUIT OF DISCIPLINE

We love stories like Rick Rescorla's because they romanticize discipline. The picture of manhood we have been sold is of a lonely man, asserting his will against a hostile world. But Rick Rescorla was a military man. He was the product of a system of discipline, and that system involved other people. We often view war heroes as models of manhood because of the great courage they display. But great men are often shaped by systems created by others. And in ignoring that, we create unrealistic and destructive expectations for ourselves.

In the past few months of changing my diet, I have needed my wife's help. I don't eat alone; I eat with my family, and my wife often cooks our meals. I wanted to help her understand why I needed to change, to give her a vision of the long-term good that I was pursuing. My pursuit of discipline doesn't simply involve my own life; it entangles everyone around me and forces them to adjust accordingly. But if we are to cultivate disciplined hearts, we must also create systems of discipline.

It was a difficult process. My wife had to make sacrifices to help me get disciplined, and even gave up some foods that she enjoyed eating because I couldn't have them. And I had to make sacrifices as well. I had to put my short-term pleasures on the altar of the long-term good of my health. But without my wife's willingness to change, the slow work of transformation would have gone on even longer.

Most men have stopped trying and have settled for a life devoid of discipline, which can only lead to stunted personal growth and little freedom. That's partly because they try to change alone. But we can't enact discipline alone; it's too dangerous. Alone we are all guaranteed failure. Alone we are almost guaranteed discouragement. The more we try, the more difficult it becomes to change, as the habit of trying and failing becomes familiar to us. The temptation to believe we are simply losers will creep in, and our motivation to continue will erode.

Very few men are able to discipline themselves without

the assistance of others. The problem with those who achieve discipline alone is that they often end up alone. Because they have succeeded, they have no empathy for those who struggle. I know a guy who is self-made, very successful, and is now influencing many people. But his standards are so high and his track record so stellar, he just doesn't believe anyone is as good as he is. He really believes that he doesn't have any peers and often belittles those who are not as successful as he is. He often says to other leaders, "You will have no friends." Because this man believes he is solely responsible for his own success, those who are near him constantly feel belittled and inferior. As a result he has no friends.

This disciplined freedom first takes shape in us. We start to doubt our emotional impulses that take us away from true masculinity. We then begin to make hard choices about our free time, focusing on the habits that will ultimately bring transformation. And we bring others whose lives are bound up in ours into that process, working with them to reimagine our lives and asking for their help. Then we begin to see results, which can motivate us to allow the practices of discipline to spill over into untouched parts of our character and skills.

The fruit of such discipline can rescue, inspire, and equip other people, as seen in Rick Rescorla's story. We never know when we will be called to step up and take responsibility for others. But when that day comes, we don't want to only try hard, but to have trained wisely. Our souls are in peril every day. We are crafting them, whether we realize it or not, as we strive to become the sort of men whose lives are flourishing and rooted in discipline.

FOUR

LOVE YOUR WORK: BECOME A WORKING MAN

WORK: THE THING YOU MAKE
OR DO BECAUSE IT'S WORTH
DOING AND BECAUSE YOU WON'T
BE HAPPY NOT DOING IT

I WAS FIRED FROM THE FIRST THREE JOBS I HAD. THE first was as a lawn mower, the second a busboy, and the third as a stock boy at a grocery store. Though the circumstances were different, the reason for each firing was the same: I was lazy. I was only working for the money, so I just endured my jobs and consequently did poorly.

Juxtapose that with my current job. I love it! I have a difficult time not working. I enjoy it; and quite frankly, I am bored when I am not working.

When it comes to their weekends, men tend to fall into one of two ditches: some guys work *for* the weekend, and others *through* the weekend.

Those who work for the weekend endure their jobs to escape into their hobbies, their yards, or their couches. For these guys, Monday through Friday are days only there to be tolerated. They are simply drudgery on the way to the utopia of a workless weekend. Weekends are where most men try to relive college, sans the classes.

Men who work *through* the weekend can't quench their need to produce. They are slaves to their e-mail and held captive by their stupid smartphones. They fear getting behind or getting fired. They are climbing the ladder, and that ladder doesn't disappear at five on Fridays. The long tentacles of their work reach into every part of their lives.

Men have a problem with work. We don't understand how to integrate our jobs into the rest of our lives. But true manhood means more than punching the clock or simply climbing the ladder. True men learn to love their work well.

WORKING AS CULTIVATION

Three of the world's major religions all look to an ancient story of creation that the Bible relays to us in Genesis. At the heart of the ancient story is a conflict between humanity and their work. In the third chapter of the book, Adam and Eve famously decided to act as their own bosses. Rather than trust that God's decisions were best for them, they gave themselves over to self-sufficiency and selfishness. As a result of all this, which Christian theology calls *sin,* men found their work more difficult and burdensome.[1] The idea is that the ground rebels against men the way they had rebelled against God (Gen. 3:16–19).

It's easy to identify with Genesis 3—work became drudgery, marriage became a chore, and Murphy's Law reigned. But things didn't begin that way. In chapter 2, God gave work to Adam before sin broke the world. God commanded him to keep the land and to cultivate it. Adam's role wasn't to build his own empire, to machete his way through a foreign wilderness in order to plant his flag on it. Instead the text indicates that God was with him in his work, seemingly working in and through it. Adam was an apprentice to the Creator of all things. His role was to cultivate the place he had been given.

Adam was a type of *vice-regent,* an old word that basically means "subking."[2] The whole world was given to Adam to steward. It was his to tend and care for because God gave it to him. But as its caretaker, Adam had a *duty* toward the land. He could have left it lying there, untouched and uncultivated. Or he could bring the best out of the land, tending the garden and contributing to the world's goodness. Before sin broke things up, work wasn't drudgery but disciplined delight.

Delightful is not the word many of us use to describe our jobs. We don't feel that we contribute, but we are forced to endure our work. We aren't cultivating; we are just coasting. We aren't making a difference; we are simply paying the bills. As the text in Genesis reminds us, the ground around us is thorny and the soil is barren. Our work works against us. It doesn't cooperate. The biblical situation still holds today: our work is cursed.

But we can take another path besides that of bitter frustration. Despite the hardness of the soil and the pain of the thorns, we can contribute and make good things. We can take the soil and make it better. We can begin to delight in our jobs. Good fruit can grow because of our efforts, fruit that brings joy and happiness to others and to ourselves.

We tend to see our work as disconnected from the rest of our lives. We live in two worlds, and what we do in one has nothing to do with how we live in the other. But what if our jobs are a training ground? What if our jobs are preparation for a bigger and better life?

> **DRILL:** List five things you love about your job. If you don't feel gratitude for the work you are able to do, then write out a paragraph saying so and why not.

The virtues we need to work well are the same we need to love our spouses well. In work, we take raw materials and draw potential out of them. That takes diligence, perseverance, care, and thoughtfulness. But any man who is diligent in thinking of his wife—who perseveres in pursuing her, who cares for her—will have a flourishing marriage. The old Norse word for *husband* literally means "one who draws out of the soil the riches that are buried there."[3]

Likewise, our work can prepare us to be better parents. A good parent recognizes potential in his child and then works for eighteen years—or longer—to help his child discover it. Our frustration with the lack of cooperation from others at work prepares us well for the "terrible twos" of a toddler or the cocky rebellion of a teenager. And the same process also happens in reverse: when we see the responsibility that we have toward others (our wives, kids, and friends), we are moved to work hard and provide for those who depend upon us. We learn the sort of virtues in our relationships that we need to work well.

A WORKING ORIENTATION

The curse on our work doesn't simply condemn work for a man; it also reveals the purpose of a man. The curse on men suggests that their functional struggle and stress are mainly associated with their jobs. Men are made for more than work. They are made to play, to have families, to embrace friendships. But beneath all that is a calling to make something of the world—a calling that burdens men and keeps them up at night.

Men struggle to subdue the ground and cultivate it in such a way that we bring out its full potential. That doesn't mean a man can't or shouldn't change diapers and wash dishes. We can and we should, especially when doing so serves our wives and children well. My point is that a man's emotional orientation is inevitably going to be toward his job. When things are off-kilter there, everything else will suffer.[4]

A man's temptation is either to hate his job or love it too much—to demonize or idolize it. He either begrudges the work and avoids it or allows it to become his master. But a truly free man knows the limits of his work. He is not free from work, but free to work well. The work

A MAN'S TEMPTATION IS EITHER TO HATE HIS JOB OR LOVE IT TOO MUCH—TO DEMONIZE OR IDOLIZE IT.

serves him and brings out the best in him, rather than destroying him or taking over. He works because the work brings him joy and because he finds it good. The slave, on the other hand, can never embrace his work in the same way because he has no choice but to do his job. We don't have to idolize or demonize our work; we can make it matter without making ourselves crazy.

THE ABSENCE OF AMBITION

One summer my dad got me a job working construction with a bunch of Vietnam War veterans. I had learned a great deal in my first two years of college, but let's just say I received a more *practical* education from these men. I learned about sacrifice, doing things right, and working from before the sun came up until there was no daylight. And as these hardworking men told me their respective stories, I learned about the consequences of bad choices and the pain that comes from unhealed wounds.

Probably the most important thing I learned while nailing down plywood came from the owner of the company, when I overheard him talk about me to a subcontractor. The owner said, "Yeah, Darrin is going to go back to college and study much harder so he doesn't have to do this crap for a living." He was right. That experience lit a fire under me to pursue a career rather than just a job, to return to school and study, *really* study, and not just coast.

I have observed three types of men when it comes to work: the settler, the driver, and the rebel. The settler has found a job but not a calling. He may be earning a comfortable income and doing good work, but he's lodged somewhere near middle management without any desire to advance. His only way forward is for others to retire. The settler is not particularly ambitious; he's found his role in life and is sticking to it. He has settled in. Settlers may see glimmers of a deeper, more fulfilling life. But they don't have frustrated ambitions because they don't have any ambition at all. And they don't struggle with overwork because they don't care much about their work. They are punching the clock and have tricked themselves into believing that this is all they were made for.

ARE YOU A SETTLER, DRIVER, OR REBEL?

Then there is the driver. Though not engaged in organized crime, drivers adopt a mafia mentality. The job comes before the family, before relationships, before everything. They're consumed with building their businesses, their 401(k)s, or accumulating piles of possessions. Or they just work to win, empowered by the idea of beating certain numbers or defeating their competition. They live for their jobs because there is nothing else to live for.

Drivers waste all their ambition on winning and accumulating, sometimes exhausting themselves and everyone around them in the process. They spend every last drop of their ambition to reach the top, and once they get there they have to fight to keep anyone from joining them. They are often unhappy until they finish climbing their particular ladder, which delivers a slice of satisfaction along with a bigger slice of loneliness.

The rebel is usually a member in good standing of hipster nation, an alternative country that resists the corporatism of America. If they have ambition—and many of these men do not—they express it outside the context of their paid employment. They are like Tyler Durden's army from *Fight Club*.

In one scene at a fund-raiser for a politician who is going to shut down the fight clubs, Durden's army corners him inside a bathroom. Brad Pitt, who plays Tyler Durden, threatens the politician, saying, "We cook your meals. We haul your trash. We connect your calls. We drive your ambulances. We guard you while you sleep. Do not [mess] with us."[5] An army of service industry guys who had settled in their jobs were bored to death and needed an outlet, so they chose fighting. Some bored men play in a band. Others choose sports leagues. Some do fantasy sports or play video games. They do whatever it takes to feel alive in the middle of dead-end jobs.

Rebels generally have divided lives; their passions and their work don't align. The jobs they really want perhaps won't pay the bills, and maybe these men are too nervous to leave behind the security of a steady income. But their frustration is real. They know they aren't doing what they were made to do. They just don't know how to get where they need to be.

EMBRACING THE GOODS OF EXPLORATION

I live in St. Louis, the "Gateway to the West." When the United States was expanding, St. Louis was originally a frontier town. The collision between the settlers and Native Americans was out of control until the city was established. As in many frontier areas, order emerged slowly out of chaos. Eventually the city opened up the great unknown of the frontier and became the fourth largest in the nation.[6]

Many settlers stayed in St. Louis rather than exploring farther west. It was an understandable choice. The Oregon Trail was dangerous, and St. Louis offered the option of living on the border of the wilderness without having to actually enter it.

> **DRILL:** What are the projects you can take up to improve your productivity at work and expand your company's value? What is broken at work that you can fix? Set a goal on your calendar for three months from now to propose a solution to your bosses.

It's risky to pursue something we don't have, because we risk losing what we do have. When it comes to our work, it's easy to stay comfortable and to stop pursuing new challenges. It is much more comfortable to find a patch of land, work it, and never risk discovering what's over the hill.

There is nothing wrong with settling into a good land and cultivating it, but there is something destructive about having a settler's spirit—the mind-set that exploration is something other people do and adventure is quarantined to movies and books. For instance, working for a municipality or state government doing road construction is a noble job. Cities need roads for businesses to operate and for people to travel. But settling for being the guy who turns the Stop and Slow sign and never seeking more responsibility would be a tragedy. No one would question the importance of this job, but it doesn't demand much out of those who fulfill it. As work, it pays the bills. But our work can do more than put food on the table; it can expand us and broaden our horizons.

Killing off the settler's spirit and awakening the possibility there could be

> IT'S RISKY TO PURSUE SOMETHING WE DON'T HAVE, BECAUSE WE RISK LOSING WHAT WE DO HAVE.

more to our lives will help us pursue both meaningful work and meaning *in* our work.

EMBRACING JOBS WE WERE NOT MADE FOR

Most men say they don't enjoy their jobs because they don't feel alive while doing them. My response to this is pretty simple: quit and do something you love. This is a real option. No one is putting a gun to your head and forcing hot, caffeine-laden coffee down your throat to get you to work every day. You really can pursue something else.

If you don't love what you're doing, find a way to quit and go do something you do love. And if what you love doesn't make any money right now, apply your creative energy to figuring out how it could. Set your mind to work on the problem as if it were a puzzle you have to solve to save your life. As they say, if you find something you love to do, you won't have to work a day in your life.

Take James, whom I met when he was a confused college student. As we discussed his uncertainties surrounding what he should do, I asked him a question I often put to young men: "If money wasn't an object and you knew you couldn't fail, what would you do?" "Start an arts center that would help the community," he said without hesitation. And so the Luminary was born, an independent nonprofit organization that exists to serve the artists of his city. Instead of just getting a comfortable job and toying with his dream, he pursued it.

Or take my friend David Karandish, who is a self-described computer nerd. David had a great idea and a passion to create an innovative business that filled a need in the burgeoning Internet commerce market. David took a risk, gathered investors, launched Announce Media, and is now winning awards and feeding families.[7]

Whether it's business, social work, or the arts, sometimes men need to leave behind their security and comfort. Yes, it is a risk. And it needs to be considered carefully, as all risks do. If you have a wife and children depending on your income, then your first priority is to take care of them. But sometimes high risk can equal high reward.

Big risks often take a long time to prepare for. Your current, less-than-perfect job could be building your character for the job you were made for. Sure, there are a lot of people who are born on third and think they've hit a triple. They fell into the right job because of their parents, connections, or social status. But for many of us, it's a long journey to the place where our jobs and our passions align. Many men want the glory of having a final position but don't want to go through the training it takes to be ready for it. It is easy to believe that the most successful men woke up in a place where their jobs and passions aligned, without realizing the long and difficult road that many of them traveled on the way.

Realizing we are in training through the various jobs we hold in life helps us let go of the idea that every job should be perfect. There is no wasted job. There is no unrighteous task if we are being formed, prepared, and equipped in every job we hold. Younger men have a strong tendency to feel entitled to the jobs they want, when they want them. Many of you were told you could be anything you wanted to be if you had a college education. Yet reality is setting in, and it hurts. Recent college graduates are struggling to find work.[8] Many are not prepared for the humility that starting at the bottom takes. The path toward finding a satisfying job is often both long and arduous.

But your less-than-perfect job is helping hone your passions. It is shoring up weaknesses in your skill set and helping you overcome deficiencies in your character. You are being sharpened like an ax so you can cut down bigger trees. You are not just working a job; you are being worked on through your job so you can learn exactly who you are and discover what you really want.

> YOUR LESS-THAN-PERFECT JOB IS HELPING HONE YOUR PASSIONS. IT IS SHORING UP WEAKNESSES IN YOUR SKILL SET AND HELPING YOU OVERCOME DEFICIENCIES IN YOUR CHARACTER.

Whatever our occupations, the heart of manliness means cheerfully taking responsibility for our lives and for those around us. That can happen in any job, even ones that don't immediately fit our passions. And the more we take responsibility, the more we will become men who are respected and rewarded for our contributions to the world.

DON'T WASTE YOUR UNEMPLOYMENT

They called it the "man-cession."[9] During the economically recessed period from December 2007 until June 2009, men lost more than two times as many jobs as women. While things have turned around a little, the trend raised concerns about whether men were prepared to face the difficult economic environment. Unemployment is difficult for anyone to face. It makes you question your worth. But it is something that many of us need to learn how to face.

Some guys are fearful *in* unemployment. Other guys are fearful *of* unemployment.

This is why many guys don't know how to retire. When guys quit working, they die sooner. When men have a job to do, they will stick around long enough to do it.

But when someone becomes unemployed or retires, his foundations are exposed. It brings key questions to the surface: Who am I? What have I been doing? What have I been giving myself to? Has it been *worth* it? Some guys can't enter retirement well because their jobs are all they've lived for, and if they don't have those, there's no reason to keep going.[10]

Any man is going to struggle if he loses his job. But some of us take it harder than others: some men are devastated. Their entire world crumbles and they don't know how to handle themselves, to the point of drowning in suicidal thoughts. Their sense of stability evaporates as the one thing by which they had measured their worth and well-being goes away.

The truth is that unemployment is an opportunity. It's a chance for us to do the hard work of evaluating our relationships to our jobs and to discern whether we have become too attached to them. It challenges us to see whether we have made our work into a god and whether we have allowed our job titles to determine our worth.

It's also an opportunity to rethink our lives and take steps toward fulfilling our callings rather than simply settling for what we had before. Some men waste their unemployment. They see the severance check as opportunity to take an extended vacation, playing at home rather than hustling to find a new job. But escaping through travel doesn't get us any closer to the goal of finding meaningful work. Other men go through unemployment in a self-induced emotional coma, unresponsive to the world around them because of their frustration with their situations. Such a sense of helplessness is difficult to face, but the moment we recognize the lie behind it is the moment we will begin to be free of the lie's effects.

In the movie *Up in the Air*, George Clooney's character makes a living firing people. In one memorable scene, Clooney has to fire an employee who had been a lifer at his company. As the employee complains, Clooney points out that children love actors because they follow their dreams—and that the French culinary undergraduate degree and the experience of bussing tables on the employee's résumé suggests that he once had interests he had never pursued. Clooney is ruthless: "How much did they first pay you to give up on your dreams?"[11] Our hopes for our lives come with a cost, and many of us are tempted to sell them for far below what they are actually worth. We don't see the slow decay of our souls very easily because we are tempted by the pursuit of a big paycheck. But to be satisfied and deeply fulfilled in our work is a great gift that few of us have the courage to pursue.

Unemployment doesn't have to be the end; it's a wake-up call, a challenge to overcome and an opportunity to orient ourselves and our work around their proper goals.

WORK AND OTHER PEOPLE

It's no secret that men are competitive. It is in our genes. My son has been competing since he got out of the womb. Whether it was battling for attention with his three sisters, fighting his neighborhood buddies with homemade swords, or taking his Little League game way too seriously, every aspect of his life is a competition.

Some men, though, are overly competitive in their work. They want to trample on others. "It's a dog-eat-dog world," they tell themselves as an excuse. But our ambition should never come at other people's expense. We do not need to cultivate a general, universal ambition or an endless desire for advancement regardless of the people whom we step on. Instead, we should be selectively ambitious. We take what is ours with gusto, fulfilling our roles with as much eagerness as we can. Even the jobs that have been given to us need to be "taken" by us; that is, seized and done with excellence fueled by masculine ambition.

Flip around the perspective for a second and imagine what it's like to work with excessively ambitious people. In an environment founded on competition and destroying others to get ahead, it is tempting to undermine our closest rivals and make their lives terrible. It's easy for those at the top of the food chain to use their power to stay there and keep other people from reaching it. Especially when one's own job is at stake. It's hard to train your replacement.

But that's functionally what All-Star major leaguer Matt Holliday did during the off-season after the Cardinals won the World Series. Holliday paid out of pocket for the top five position-playing prospects in the Cardinals organization to work out with him and other veterans. He put them up in a nice hotel, paid for their meals, and most important, spent time with them so they could experience St. Louis and learn the "Cardinal way." Holliday basically offered to help and bless some of the men who will one day take his job.[12]

Matt Holliday isn't a hero for that. He's simply doing what he should be doing. He's making his work inclusive of other people, bringing them into it and passing along what he knows to those who have less experience. He's mentoring, leading, and challenging younger players to fulfill their talents and their abilities.

THE SACRIFICE OF WORK

One of the main reasons guys resent their jobs is because they require them to sacrifice, to lay down their wants and preferences for the greater good of the organization. We don't want our low-maintenance, hassle-free lives to be disturbed. We don't want to be interrupted, to have the neatness and cleanliness of our lives confronted by the messiness that invariably results when organizations go after big things.

Or we don't want to share the glory with others. It's easy to check out of work if we are being overlooked while others on the team are being lauded. Some men resent their work because their egos haven't been satisfied with the attention they've received.

Some of us are in the difficult position of not truly believing in our organization's goals. Working for a company like that may provide the satisfaction of paying the bills and supporting the family, but it also creates a divide between our deepest desires to do something meaningful and the way we spend the majority of our time.

Finding satisfaction in our work demands a lot from us, and we will have to sacrifice something. We must deal a death-blow to our sense of comfort, our unholy ambition, and our desire to crush other people. We must not live beneath our privilege and give in to the desire to simply pay the bills without thinking about what sort of value we're bringing into the world through our efforts.

FIVE

GET SATISFACTION: BECOME A CONTENT MAN

CONTENTMENT: LEARNING TO SAY
"WELL DONE" AND "ENOUGH"

MY FAMILY RECENTLY MOVED INTO A NEW HOUSE EVEN though we hadn't quite sold our old one yet. Though our new house was better in every conceivable way, my family missed the old house, the only one our children had known. My wife wisely suggested that we visit the old house and close out that chapter of our lives. So we returned and did a ritual. We entered each room and told stories. We remembered good times and hard times and all the little things in between.

The kids each went into part of their bedrooms and wrote their names in discreet places. My children needed a sense of completion in order to enjoy their new home. They needed to look back and reflect on their lives, to be appreciative and thankful for the good they had experienced during that season. Without that time, they were never going to be content in their new circumstance because they had not found closure on the previous season of their lives.

In our culture there are few, if any, rituals of celebration that commemorate the passing of one stage of manhood to the next. We don't know how to find closure, which makes finding satisfaction difficult. Think of the Jewish bar mitzvah, which closes out adolescence at the age of thirteen and inaugurates manhood. It creates a clear set of social expectations for the new man. New roles and responsibilities are established that everyone in the community recognizes and acknowledges. But it also provides a sense of completeness to a young man's childhood.

David Arquette, a B-list celebrity who is best known for marrying Courteney Cox, had a bar mitzvah at the Wailing Wall in June 2012 and summed up the experience well: "Finally I'm a man."[1] The rest of us have no road map to our lives, no path we can follow that will help us know when we've arrived. And that makes the search for satisfaction impossible. We're looking for treasure without a map.

Don Draper is the man many men think they want to be. The main character of the hit show *Mad Men,* he has an insatiable sexual desire accompanied by an unparalleled ability to get women. He is partner at his firm, drinks all day, and still manages to be at the top of his world. He has his struggles, of course; his life seems to be constantly teetering on the edge of total self-destruction. But somehow he always escapes.

As an advertising executive, it's Draper's job to understand what people want—and how to make them want new things. He sells happiness. Where happiness already exists, Draper sows discontentment so people will buy what he's selling.

We have all heard the call to be content, that we should accept our lot in life and enjoy what we have. But the world we live in is set up to deepen our discontentment. We have been told the *what* ("Be content!") but not the *how* ("Hey, here are a few things you can do to actually become more content!"). And we definitely haven't been told why we should want contentment. Usually people think it is self-evident. After all, who *wouldn't* want to be satisfied?

Turns out, we don't want to be content. We keep buying more stuff and doing more things. The striving is endless. The pile of gadgets grows, and the desire for bigger houses, nicer cars, and a cooler wardrobe is insatiable.

Contentment means not only saying, "Enough," but also saying, "Well done." It is the ability to rest in the knowledge that our participation and production in this life have been good. Contentment comes from the person, not circumstances or possessions. It is about who we are as men rather than what we have collected.

Developing a sense of contentment means entering into rituals of reflection and celebration of the various stages of our lives. If life is only one big, long story and we never pause to celebrate the various chapters, then our awareness of the good we have done will be vague, and our discontentment will grow. Contentment is the sort of thing that must be practiced if it is to be realized.

> CONTENTMENT MEANS NOT ONLY SAYING, "ENOUGH," BUT ALSO SAYING, "WELL DONE."

THE PURPOSE OF CONTENTMENT

To say that contentment has a purpose seems contradictory. After all, isn't being content the destination itself? In a sense, we don't need a reason to pursue contentment—it is the reason we do everything we do. As the French mathematician Blaise Pascal wrote:

> All men seek happiness. This is without exception. Whatever different means they employ, they all tend to this end. The cause of some going to war, and of others avoiding it, is the same desire in both, attended with different views. The will never takes the least step but to this object. This is the motive of every action of every man, even of those who hang themselves.[2]

We do everything we do in life to be happy and content. But because we don't seem to be very content as men, we need to reflect a little more deeply about what contentment is and what it will actually bring us. At the heart of contentment is an embrace of the present and a willingness to enjoy the good things we have right now. Contentment is freedom from the cares of the past and concerns for the future.

Today, as I sit writing, it is a cool summer morning and the birds congregating around the bird feeder my family recently put up are alternatively singing and fighting. It's a beautiful morning—a truly good day that needs to be enjoyed. Throughout this writing process, I've struggled to be content with my life. I face pressure to get it done, to reach the destination of "having written." I could let those pressures erode my enjoyment of the world. But contentment, the freedom to simply embrace the gifts around us, is worth warding off all distractions.

R. C. Sproul Jr., a pastor and teacher, recently lost his wife to cancer. When he was asked what he regretted, his answer was devastatingly straightforward: "I wish I would have held her hand more."[3] For married men, the practice of holding hands with our wives builds contentment. You can't hurry if you're holding hands. It's not simply about getting to the destination; it's about being with each other on the way. Similarly, I often tell young men to enjoy their youth and be grateful for it. Not because I think we should idolize youthfulness and strive to stay in that stage for the rest of our lives, but because enjoying the moment is like working a muscle: if we strengthen it early, it will be strong for the long haul.

Contentment isn't automatic or inevitable. It won't simply happen when our circumstances change or if we reach our goals. Contentment must become a part of our character and woven throughout the fabric of our lives.

BOREDOM AND CONTENTMENT

As a kid, I would do anything for excitement. I wanted to experience the thrills of feeling alive. I was perpetually bored, as are many of you. And part of the reason for that was I hadn't bothered to notice my surroundings.

When I left for college, I knew nothing about topography. I had rarely thought about it growing up in southern Illinois, and I remember being amazed at how different my little college town was from where I had been raised. Only after moving away did I realize that I missed the amazing lakes, cliffs, and even the trees. In my boredom, I ignored the beauty of God's creation around me.

Bored people don't know what they're living for, in part because they aren't enjoying what they have. I see this in my children every summer when school lets out. For most of the year, school structures their lives and provides them with a sense of purpose. They have to read books; they want to earn their parents' and teachers' approval; they care about the work they are doing. But when all that ends, they are left aimless and directionless—and they invariably get bored.

BORED PEOPLE DON'T KNOW WHAT THEY'RE LIVING FOR, IN PART BECAUSE THEY AREN'T ENJOYING WHAT THEY HAVE.

Contentment eludes men who are consumed by a restless ambition. It's impossible to relax and be content in the moment if we're consumed by striving for the next thing. David Brooks described the conundrum for a certain sort of college student a decade ago in his essay "The Organization Kid."[4] These kids are always going, always on the run, always trying to beef up their résumés so they can achieve all their dreams. But the problem is that once they "arrive," they find themselves no more content than they were on the journey.

ASSASSINS OF CONTENTMENT

Contentment has a target on its back. Dynamics at work within us seek to kill it. If we are going to find satisfaction, we need to fight off the assassins of contentment and embrace practices and rhythms that build contentment in us. Such assassins distract us from the present and prompt us to either idolize or demonize our past and future. We either worship or hate the past or future, but doing so makes it impossible to embrace the glory of the contented life.

Regret

The regrets men carry can be very real and debilitating to our contentment. Sometimes we *should* regret things. If we make bad decisions, if we hurt other people, we need to acknowledge our mistakes and feel their weight.

But some men allow their regrets to turn into a cancer of self-loathing that undermines their ability to make balanced and healthy stories out of their lives. Regret, left unchecked, will leave you in a state of helplessness and erode contentment.

SOME MEN ALLOW THEIR REGRETS TO TURN INTO A CANCER OF SELF-LOATHING THAT UNDERMINES THEIR ABILITY TO MAKE BALANCED AND HEALTHY STORIES OUT OF THEIR LIVES.

Nostalgia

Some people won't ever enjoy the present because they idolize the past. Whether it was in childhood, college, or a previous city in which they lived, some men can't escape the successes and joys of the past or welcome those of the present. Nostalgia suffocates our ability to enjoy our lives because we can never escape the unrealistic burden of having to measure our lives according to a standard set a year or decade ago.

Fear

Some people are so consumed by their fear of what will come tomorrow that they cannot embrace today. They worry that if they enjoy something a little too much, they will be devastated if it goes away. As a result, people who are consumed by fear are always hedging their bets, always pulling back at the last second from the edge of truly enjoying life.

Vision

To have vision for the future is a good thing, but some men are so distracted by theirs that they can't embrace the present. These men can't appreciate the life they have now because they're waiting to achieve their goals so that their lives will finally turn around. They're intoxicated by their preferred future, drunk on the possibilities before them. The problem, though, is that while waiting for tomorrow, they don't really live today.

Multitasking

If you're trying to do everything at any given moment, there's a good chance that you're not doing anything. Multitasking spreads our attention across a hundred activities, meaning that we can't fully engage in any one of them. Surprisingly, this erodes contentment because we rarely allow ourselves the pleasure of the feeling of completion. When we multitask, it is difficult to give ourselves over to our work completely and experience the intrinsic reward of seeing it to its end.

Overexposure

For men, overexposure happens most obviously when we look at pornography. It's harder to appreciate the female body if we are constantly looking at it naked. The wonder and enchantment men feel about women is wrapped up with a sense of mystery. Placing limits on what we see helps keep that sense in place.

Pornography also destroys a man's contentment because it gives him unrealistic expectations about how women look and what they can and should do. A real woman, according to TV commercials, should have a perfect body while eating a calorie-laden fast-food hamburger. Really? Studies demonstrate that men who oversaturate themselves with images of beautiful women become less content in their marriages and are tricked into thinking they deserve better.[5] Overexposure undermines contentment from nearly every direction.

Hurriedness

Business is doing all the things that we are responsible for, but hurriedness is the frantic mental and emotional state we experience while doing them. It's impossible to enjoy doing what we're supposed to do when we are hurried. We can't celebrate anything because we don't give ourselves any space to realize that it is good. We simply want to get on to the next thing on the list.

LEARNING THE RHYTHMS
OF CONTENTMENT

Many of us tend to distrust structures and routines. But structure is helpful for much of life, specifically with regard to contentment. The presence of fluid structure and rhythm nurtures contentment by helping us know where we are going and what we should be doing at any given moment.

We shouldn't seek a structure simply to produce more or get through our task lists. A healthy structure protects us from worrying where our lives are headed or what we're going to do next. A good structure allows us to enjoy the moment without relapsing into laziness, because we know that when our current task is completed we will be able to move on to the next one in a healthy way. Structure also allows us not to give in to workaholism because we have predetermined how much focus to give particular tasks.

The rhythms of contentment, though, also involve rhythms of work and rest. They require both working hard and resting well. Some parents teach their kids to work but don't encourage them to play. Other parents only encourage their kids to play but don't teach them to work. But we have to do both. Our work is central to our manhood. It is something we have been (as we've seen) made to do, something to be embraced willingly and joyfully. But we have to rest well to work well; the rest completes and perfects the work itself.

Rituals of celebration and rest after we have worked well are essential for building up the memory bank of contentment and, consequently, fueling our future contentment. The more we step back and enjoy what we have accomplished, the more prone we will be to accomplish more. Contentment fuels work, which fuels more contentment. Resting well doesn't mean just checking out and not doing anything. It simply means delighting and rejoicing in a job well done by freely embracing something that isn't the job. The inability to step away from our work is a sign that it possesses us, which means we will never find the satisfaction we were made for.

DRILL: Find your most recent accomplishment at work or in your marriage. Did you celebrate it? Call your wife (if you have one) or a friend and take her or him out to dinner as a belated celebration. And then invite your wife or friend to celebrate his or her latest accomplishment too.

CONTENTMENT AND OUR PAIN

Over the past few years, I have dealt with a number of health problems. I've had chronic back pain, a handful of auto-immune diseases, and trouble sleeping. Some of you have dealt with much worse. We don't have to look too hard to find men who have suffered more than us and yet have the kind of contentment we envy. The real test of manhood is whether a man can suffer while continuing to enjoy the good in and around his life.

Suffering makes us hyperaware of the things we take for granted. You don't appreciate bending over until you can't do it without stabbing pain. Suffering also prods us to want to be well.

We don't have to wait for suffering to wake us up in order to notice the world around us. We have the choice to notice and enjoy. But most of us do wait until we experience a pain before we start realizing just how good we had it all along. As C. S. Lewis put it,

> WE DON'T HAVE TO WAIT FOR SUFFERING TO WAKE US UP IN ORDER TO NOTICE THE WORLD AROUND US. WE HAVE THE CHOICE TO NOTICE AND ENJOY.

pain is "[God's] megaphone to rouse a deaf world."[6] It wakes us up from our slumber and forces us to confront ourselves and the good we enjoy.

THE GODLIKE QUALITY OF BEING SATISFIED

The Bible opens with a story about how God created the world. It's a story that sets the pattern for the rest of the Bible, as it is the introduction to who God is and what he wants for humanity. What's fascinating, though, is that while the Bible presents God as a being who is capable of arranging the cosmos, it also demonstrates that he knows when to stop. After spending six days creating the world, Genesis says that God declared his work "very good" and then spent a seventh day resting from his work before he began ruling over his work (Gen. 1:31).

Even God steps back and celebrates a job well done. He pauses to acknowledge the goodness of his creation. He doesn't hurry on to the next thing, to check off the next item on his infinite task list. Instead he delights in his work and experiences the contentment we are promised.

EVEN GOD KNOWS WHEN TO STOP AND CELEBRATE.

The Bible suggests, in fact, that we are to imitate God's willingness to pause for a day and rejoice in our work. God establishes a limit on our activities when he commands humanity to spend one day a week resting. We are not made to work every minute of every week, much less every day.

Those limits aren't restrictive. They are there for our good, to remind us that we do not control every part of our lives, and they allow us the freedom to celebrate our work. We can't control the future; we can only decide each moment how we will embrace the world around us. Nor can we go back and change the past; we can only begin to cultivate contentment from this moment forward by stepping back from our lives and appreciating them for what they are.

Contentment is godlike. It is a quality that goes to the heart of true manliness—that sets a man above the world and elevates him to a level few attain. The contented life is a powerful life, for it means recognizing and staying within our limits and embracing our work and our pleasure with equal gusto. It is a powerful life because it recognizes that contentment is a quality of the soul and not our circumstances, and it enables us to find good in the midst of pain and suffering that few others can see.

There's an old story of a fellow who, during some difficult circumstances, had the wisdom to see that he could still be content. "I just know, when I get to heaven and think back at my old life," he would say, "I'm going to have this thought: If I knew how great it was, I would have enjoyed it more." There is a temptation for us to become that guy. And that is a temptation we should fight.

SIX

LOVE A WOMAN: BECOME A DEVOTED MAN

DEVOTION: PASSIONATELY
PURSUING A GOOD AND LETTING
NOTHING STAND IN OUR WAY

"LET ME BE THE FIRST TO SAY CONGRATULATIONS TO you. You can have one woman the rest of your life."

So says Vince Vaughn's character in the frat comedy *Old School,* only he doesn't say "woman." In an uncomfortably comical scene, he attempts to talk his friend (Will Ferrell) out of getting married—while Ferrell is standing at the altar, watching his future bride walk down the aisle.[1] The line sums up how we have been trained to think about marriage.

Before I met my wife, I was quite promiscuous. I slept with my girlfriends and then cheated on them. I remember talking with a close friend before I got married about how I had no idea how I was going to survive having sex with only one woman until the day I died.

For many young men, manliness means conquering as many women as they can with as few consequences as possible. Tucker Max, the frat boy who wrote a book containing his tales of sexual exploits, has created an army of imitators who approach women with the sole purpose of sleeping with them. In January 2011, two Princeton alumni and a State Department employee were outed for running a competition to see who could have the most sex.[2] A student in a frat at USC sent an e-mail to the whole group, suggesting that women were "targets."[3] And it's not just guys anymore: one girl made a PowerPoint presentation of the guys she had slept with at Duke, rating them for their appearance and sexual performance.[4]

> TOO MANY MEN HAVE BEEN CAUGHT SETTLING FOR CHEAP, DISTORTED VERSIONS OF LOVE RATHER THAN SEEKING THE REAL THING.

Every man needs help loving women, even the single guys. Too many men have been caught settling for cheap, distorted versions of love rather than seeking the real thing. I travel quite a bit for my job, and when you travel it is easy to settle for "tourist traps," which are basically counterfeits of local, authentic culture. Counterfeits are easier to find, eat at, and shop at. Tourist traps keep people from exploring the real thing, often by being flashier, noisier, and easier to get to. Many guys have become sexual tourists and have been caught in an erotic trap, getting cheap thrills that pretend to be the real thing but aren't.

The tourist trap of sexual promiscuity provides a pseudo-happiness but misses the power and depth of relationships that we are made for. As I mentioned, tourist traps in general are convenient; they're easily accessible, but less than satisfying. It takes a long time to become a local and to learn the good spots in town. But when we do, we find a texture and goodness that simply cannot be imitated. That is the sort of sexual relationship that will satisfy us our entire lives.

Think about being seventy, with children and grandchildren huddled around you as you tell stories of your youth. Previous generations of men were able to speak of defeating evil in World War II or overcoming the difficulties of the Depression. And there you are at seventy, boasting about manipulating dozens of women, giving a play-by-play account of your sexual exploits. At best, you're now a dirty old man. At worst, you're gonna land in jail. It is an easy thing, in some ways, to have sex with a woman. It is a far more challenging, rewarding, and noble thing to pursue a woman, marry her, and remain devoted to her.

Some of you reading this might think that sounds too restrictive. Devoting yourself to one woman might sound impossible. But remember the goal: it is to have a great marriage—not simply a good one—where your spouse is your best friend and you are both satisfied sexually.

Historically, men have married for social reasons and kept mistresses to fulfill their sexual passions. And some guys still approach marriage that way; they view cheating as part of a marriage and not as a problem. They think they're entitled to sex with whomever they want, and marriage isn't going to stop them from getting it. They have no intention of being a one-woman man.

But the vast majority of guys get married thinking they're going to forsake their other sexual outlets. They want to make a go of being married to one woman, even if they're not quite sure how. This chapter is for them. It's for the guys who want to love their wives but aren't sure how. It's for the guys who want to someday be one-woman men, but are worried that somewhere, deep within their hearts, they aren't quite sure they can do it.

UNMASKING FAITHFULNESS

"Mommy porn" is a relatively new term that may best be embodied by E. L. James's novel *Fifty Shades of Grey*. This novel didn't simply become popular—it is a true phenomenon, much like *Harry Potter*. Because the book can be read on Kindles and iPads, women have been able to read it discreetly. And sales have exploded. The paper edition sold more copies faster in the UK than any book in history, selling at its peak some one hundred thousand copies a week.[5]

Mommy porn is popular because men are not. The demand for such stories suggests that when it comes down to it, women are dissatisfied with their marriages and their men. They're not getting the sort of spark they once had. Couples may be living together, but they aren't devoted to each other.

Porn can be the result of having a dead marriage, but it can also kill one. It's a known fact that pornography decreases marital satisfaction, rather than increasing it.[6] Porn keeps people from passionate marriages but also conditions them so that they don't even want them. Porn is a counterfeit outlet for intimacy. It's corrosive, it creates dissatisfaction with real sexual experiences with actual women, and it destroys trust.

Porn gives guys control, which they desperately love having and which can destroy them. When our wives don't respond sexually, it forces us to acknowledge our own limitations. We are confronted with the reality that the person we are with is a *person*, not an object, and thus is not subject to our will and our whims. Some guys can't handle that, so they turn to women they can turn on and off with no more than a click—the ones on their computer screens.

Porn remains attractive to men partly from our ignorance. We reduce marriage to simply sticking together through thick and thin and being faithful to the vows we have made. That isn't bad, but it's not best. Staying married to someone is a good start, but there is something higher, something deeper, something better.

DRILL: Go to CovenantEyes.com and sign up right now. Don't hesitate. Just do it.

Many men who are faithful are not devoted. For them, *faithfulness* becomes a code word for passivity. But you can coexist with a woman without loving her. Your marriage may look good but not feel good. You may be married but only on a technicality—you are really more in a business arrangement than in love.

Being devoted, on the other hand, means transitioning from passive endurance of your marriage to passionate exploration of your wife. Passivity at home is one reason guys can be so competitive and ambitious in their work and play. The energy that is being funneled toward their jobs could be better used to explore the women to whom they have committed their lives. They're not investing in their marriages the way they do their retirement. They don't fight for romance the way they fight for their hobbies.

LOVING A WOMAN'S BEAUTY

To be a husband is to cultivate, to till the soil of a woman's heart, and to draw out and contribute to its beauty and goodness. It means patiently exploring her interests and concerns, not because you want to get your wife in the sack but because you wish to make her character beautiful.

True men devote themselves to deepening their wives' beauty. One of the main New Testament texts on marriage, Ephesians 5, speaks about how a husband is to "wash" his wife (v. 26). This sounds like something erotic, but it is far from it. In the first century, baths weren't pleasurable—they were painful. They didn't have antibacterial soap or ointment, so "giving someone a bath" often meant washing out the infection from their wounds.[7] A woman would have had to trust the man to attend to the most sensitive parts of her body. And for that to happen, a man would have to be worthy of trust.

How do you know whether you are a devoted man? Your wife talks to you about her dreams, fears, and concerns more than she talks with her mother or her friends. Your wife encourages you, rather than tearing you down. Your wife is hopeful about the future and looks forward to life together. Your wife has a sense of flourishing; her world is stable and good. Your wife's heart is soft, tender, and open to you.

If you think I'm suggesting that women are weak and frail and just waiting for men to come around and help them out, well, I'm not. Once you get to know a woman, you see how tough and strong a woman can be. Women live longer than men, and there's a longstanding impression that women have a higher pain tolerance than men.[8] And women bear children, which I have witnessed four times. Women are incredibly strong, even if their strength often looks different from men's.

Men who seek their wives and devote themselves to their beauty will never run out of things to do. A good woman can never be fully explored. She is constantly learning, growing, and changing. In devoting ourselves to one woman, we commit ourselves to a lifetime of exploring a strange, foreign, and rich land.

In marriage, both people have to be equally committed to experiencing passionate devotion together. But when that sort of devotion doesn't exist, someone needs to take the first step, just as they do when two people dance; someone has to initiate the movement and lead. To be a man is to joyfully see, own, and fulfill the responsibility on us. That doesn't mean our wives don't have responsibilities as well, or that they can't take the initiative. They can and they should. But that misses the deeper question: Why *shouldn't* men step forward in pursuing the opposite sex? If they do this within the marriage, it creates a world where women feel loved and desired, and consequently feel more empowered and free to take their own initiative and leadership. So why not men?[9]

HOLISTIC DEVOTION

What does it look like to be passionately devoted to our spouses? Holistic devotion goes beyond the bedroom, but includes the bedroom. Being a man means seeing how our sexual desires integrate with the rest of our lives. Holistic devotion has several different components.

Physical Devotion

I know everyone wants to focus on what happens between the sheets. And that makes sense: sex is the high point, the culmination of our devotion to our spouses, the consummation of the union. But every married guy eventually realizes that as the culmination of such devotion, sex actually begins way outside the bedroom and long before intercourse. It's a journey of two lives coming together, not simply an isolated act. When we give our spouses hugs when we arrive home from work and offer sympathetic and listening ears, we express the sort of devotion outside the bedroom that makes what happens in the bedroom genuine.

Guys who are one-woman men don't simply stay married to one woman. They devote all their sexual energy and attention to the woman. When girls with skirts a little too high and blouses a little too low come across our paths, true men don't yield. Their hearts *and* their eyes are for their wives, who are their standard of beauty. Literally. When men are attracted to someone, their eyes grow just a little bit larger. They may not realize it, but they're giving themselves away to those who observe them closely. Men who are married devote their eyes to their spouses, developing habits of noticing and attending to their wives so that their love and affection grow.[10]

Emotional Devotion

Anatomically, a man moves toward the woman in a sexual encounter. Likewise, the woman, in such an encounter, must open herself to receive the man. And what is true anatomically is also true emotionally. A good husband moves toward his wife, and when this is done well, the wife also receives him.

Truly moving toward your wife sexually only happens when you move toward her emotionally.

Spiritual Devotion

Remember your first roommate? Maybe it was in college. Maybe it was during your first job. But the thing about roommates is, you hate them. Okay, maybe you didn't hate them, but at some point you hated that they weren't like you. They didn't do things the way you do. They didn't clean the way you do. They didn't eat the way you do. They didn't even like the same foods you do. But at least you could leave them for days at a time without having to give them a reason. You could escape your roommate at the end of the lease or semester.

You can't escape your wife. She knows (or will know) when you lie and even why you are lying. She will remind you of your greatness and your weakness, the glory and the gore. This will crush you and heal you. She will be holy sandpaper in your life, rubbing off the things that keep you from being the man you are called to be.

> MEN WHO ARE MARRIED DEVOTE THEIR EYES TO THEIR SPOUSES, DEVELOPING HABITS OF NOTICING AND ATTENDING TO THEIR WIVES SO THAT THEIR LOVE AND AFFECTION GROW.

Defining *spirituality* turns out to be nearly impossible, so it's not really that helpful a word if you look too closely at it. But there are generally two sides to it. Spirituality either emphasizes hyperimmanence (God is near me) or hypertranscendence (God is far from me). Both of these extremes make us too focused either on our immediate experience or on our helplessness.

Marriage forces us to look at both sides, though. We have to focus on our mundane, immediate circumstances. We have to come clean to grow, to tell each other the truth and be honest with each other. There is no escaping the gritty, practical difficulties of life when we're married.

But intimacy also points to a reality beyond ourselves. It suggests that there's something greater than sex. Sex always leaves us wanting more; the contentment and pleasure inevitably melt away. That is why some guys get addicted to it—they are trying to meet spiritual cravings with sex, and sex can never meet them.

DRILL: Every relationship needs outside counsel to thrive. Go to FamilyLife.com and subscribe to their podcast. Make it a daily listen on your way to work.

INTEGRITY AND TRUE MANHOOD

Kevin is one of the leading spine surgeons in my city and a guy who is straightforward about everything. He doesn't pull punches. After he had been at his job for a while and had seen a lot of guys have affairs, he told his wife, "Honey, I'm a jerk and I work too much. I'm too nitpicky. I've got a thousand sins.

But I don't think I could ever have an affair. I just don't have the energy." Keeping up multiple credit card accounts, ensuring that the cell phone is always clean, and maintaining two totally separate lives actually is a lot of work. It takes a ton of energy— energy that could be devoted to loving our spouses better or improving at our jobs.

But guys still do it, in part because the passion makes them feel alive. They may not be honest with their spouses about their frustrations, but they'll vent with the attractive woman at work. When their legs brush inadvertently beneath the table, or their shoulders accidentally rub while walking past each other in the hall, they feel the spark, and the flame of passion begins. Feeling attracted to other people happens, but those feelings become legitimate temptations when all that energy is stored up because it hasn't been devoted to your spouse.

> NO ONE THINKS THE HEIGHT OF MASCULINITY IS A GUY SITTING AT HIS COMPUTER WITH HIS PANTS AROUND HIS ANKLES.

In short, guys go to great lengths to feel that sort of passion, including covering their tracks for everything they do. That's true of porn too. A guy has to expend a lot more energy to maintain his porn addiction. He's clearing his Internet history every time he gazes at naked chicks. He has to sneak off to find time alone. His passion for fulfilling his porn addiction will force him to make sacrifices and expend efforts to get what he wants.

All that deception covers over our true manhood, which is rooted in our integrity, our truthfulness, and our ability to simply be ourselves without hesitation or reservation regardless of the circumstances. No one thinks the height of masculinity is a married guy sneaking around his wife's back using another credit card and another cell number. And no one thinks the height of masculinity is a guy sitting at his computer with his pants around his ankles.

Men who learn to tell the truth about their lives will learn to love well. Men who live double lives may feel alive for a moment, but everything they do is for the thrill and not for the other person. When the thrill is gone, they won't be any better as men or any better fit to love another person.

THE SINGLE MAN

Being a passionate man does not mean you have to be married. Many guys now are waiting to get hitched, and some are forgoing it altogether. The average marrying age is now twenty-nine for men.[11] Either way, every guy is going to be single for at least a season of his adult life, and it's important to know how to cultivate our passions outside of our romantic lives.

Remember that, after all, what happens in sex is simply a part of life, not the whole of it. If that's true, then how we cultivate our lives will prepare us well to engage in sex—or we'll simply be better men, even if we never have sex at all.

There are a lot of single guys out there who are neither becoming interesting men nor are very focused on their lives. They're adrift, lost in a sea of pathetic jobs and video games, and uncertain about what they want to do or whom they want to be with. They're aimless, in more ways than one.

Your season as a single man is an excellent opportunity to become an interesting person, to learn about the world and find your place within it. It's a chance to get beyond the computer screen or video games and to acquire the sort of skills and interests that will hold people's attention when they're fifty as easily as they do when they're five.

Gain some skills. Learn to cook rather than simply eating out. Develop a love of reading. Learn a foreign language or two, so that when you do all your traveling, you are able to say a bit more than "hello." Take up a musical instrument, and not simply because you have visions of rock stardom but because playing music is fun. Try a new sport. Stop being so boring. Fight your fear of marriage and become the kind of man a good woman would want.

True men will never be satisfied by the thousands of pseudo-intimate experiences available to them. The women you picked up in the bar, or online, or even the virtual women of porn may provide a little recreational fun. But they are not going to be able to satisfy you in any meaningful sense.

"I enjoy sex just as much as Joe Namath." That hilarious sentence was uttered on national TV in 1975 by quarterback Roger Staubach. They were the two greatest quarterbacks of their generation. But off the field, they couldn't have been more different. Namath's reputation as a womanizer was legendary, while Staubach was a family man.

And the CBS reporter knew it, which is why she asked on national TV whether being a family man was a burden. But Staubach, with his straightforward Southern demeanor, didn't back down. "I only do it with one girl, you know?" he drawled. "But it's still fun."[12]

Joe Namath was a sexual tourist, someone who reveled in the pseudointimacy that sexual pleasure brings. And any man can do that. But it takes a true man to love a woman the way Roger Staubach did.

SEVEN

LOVE KIDS: BECOME A FAMILY MAN

FAMILY MAN: SINGLE OR MARRIED,
A MAN WHO SEES AND AFFIRMS
HIS COMMITMENT TO THOSE
WHO DEPEND ON HIM

JOE IS AN EXECUTIVE AND IS MARRIED WITH FIVE KIDS. Carlos is a single young professional. Both of them have told me on numerous occasions that since they were little boys, they have dreamed about having a family. They both daydreamed about what the kids would look like, what activities they would pursue with them, and what it would feel like to hang out with them. They pictured themselves meeting the right girl and growing old with her.

I couldn't have been more opposite. I remember thinking about kids exactly twice before I got married. Both times were when my girlfriend was "late," and I wasn't exactly jubilant. I had never held a baby for more than a couple of minutes or changed a diaper until my first child was born to my wife and me. I had to learn on the fly, building the ship while sailing it. Not a good way to go.

Truth be told, I was a little scared of kids. They were unpredictable. They screamed. They cried. They were messy. They asked awkward questions. But it wasn't just all that that made me concerned. Their presence reminded me how scared I was when I was a kid.

My parents were both born during the Great Depression. The economic hurricane almost destroyed our nation. It was so much worse than the recession that began in 2008 that comparisons are almost offensive. Growing up, Dad managed his business and Mom managed the home. Both of them worked extremely hard and were very frugal, perhaps with the memory of their childhoods in mind. As a result, my childhood was not a fun time for me. I don't remember being at ease, really being able to enjoy being a kid, which translated into my lack of desire to have children.

My friend Mark has had quite a ride in his short life. Not even thirty years old, Mark earned a scholarship to Oklahoma to play football and was able to play in the national championship. Eventually he was drafted and enjoyed several years of success. Mark signed with a new team and was having the best four games of his career. Then, on a routine pass route, Mark blew out his knee. Three surgeries and two years later, Mark is still struggling to get back on the field. But while rehabbing his physical injuries, Mark also realized he needed some rehab on his childhood.

Mark grew up in a family where emotions were to be kept to yourself. If you were happy, sad, glad, or mad, you kept it bottled up. Mark was taught to stuff his anger, fear, and even his joy. To be open made you vulnerable. His reserve greatly benefited him professionally, but it killed him relationally. You can keep your emotions bottled up on the field, but you can't do that with your wife and children.

Mark is realizing that he has to acknowledge the glory and gory of his upbringing. It isn't that Mark's family is a bunch of bad people. Mark's family was actually very helpful in helping him become a man. They simply didn't know what to do with their unwanted emotions. So they pushed them down and taught Mark to do the same. Mark is coming to grips with the fact that to have an emotionally healthy home for his wife and kids, he is going to have to be reprogrammed. What does it look like to be present with his wife? How does he empower his kids to pursue their dreams? How does he help set the emotional and spiritual tone of his home? These are the questions Mark has to ask.

THE LEAD SACRIFICER

Leading is one of the most difficult things to do in life. It's much easier to sit in the back and watch things unfold than jump on the moving train. When you follow, you can coast and you can criticize. When you follow, you can daydream about leadership. But when you lead, you stand in front and take responsibility for everyone else behind. You can't coast, complain, or fantasize if you want to lead well.

When it comes to their families and children, men tend to fall into two extremes. On the one hand, some men avoid or abdicate their responsibilities to care for those around them. They passively allow others to assume leadership or they withdraw altogether. Passive men are often nice guys, but they aren't respected because they refuse to take risks. They linger on the beach, unwilling to brave the waves. They drown out the voice that says we were made for a life of courage, love, and justice.

On the other hand, some men adopt chauvinistic and abusive attitudes toward others. They take themselves too seriously and their responsibility as leaders not seriously enough. When such abusive men are in charge, people feel neglected and uncared for. Everyone has to tread carefully so that they don't cross the leader—even if they aren't sure what the leader wants. In the family, the spouse and children must be particularly careful, as the punishment will never fit their crime. In such environments, no one can express themselves freely, but they conform to what is expected of them. Rather than helping people flourish, abusive men turn others into objects for their own self-gratification and glory—and then call it "leadership."

> PASSIVE MEN ARE OFTEN NICE GUYS, BUT THEY AREN'T RESPECTED BECAUSE THEY REFUSE TO TAKE RISKS.

Between those two is a life of leading the family through sacrificing for it. Rather than chauvinistically demanding that others meet their needs, or passively standing in the background, men can recognize other people's interests as more important and courageously deny their own desires for their family's good.

Real leadership takes courage because it means not simply doing whatever family members want. Sometimes, children want things they shouldn't have and they need to be told no. But that will only be effective if husbands and fathers have already set aside their own interests and made it clear that they care more about their children than they do themselves. If they sacrifice themselves for their families, they'll have the sort of authority that children (and wives) are naturally drawn to.

THE LEAD EXAMPLE

There was an old public service announcement where the dad finds the kid's drug stash and asks him where he learned to do drugs. The kid famously retorts, "From you, all right? I learned it by watching you!" Then the voiceover guy says in an ominous voice, "Parents who do drugs have kids who do drugs."[1]

Your family is looking to you. Literally. They are watching your every move. So what are they learning? It's important that you have standards and values and that you're modeling what it means to be a Jones or a Smith or, for my family, a Patrick. I want my kids to see that being a Patrick means something. My children's little minds and hearts are soaking up tons of information, especially in moments when my guard is down and when I don't think I'm actually teaching them. And my desire is to exemplify at all times the honesty, the care and concern, and the love that I want to mark our family.

We all know children learn by example. Which is why the most important thing that fathers can do for them is to act with integrity and courage at all times.

THE LEAD CONFESSOR

Beneath the word *confess* is a sense of togetherness: it means "to acknowledge something with someone else."[2] A man who confesses wants to remain with others. He doesn't want to be alone in his lies and deceptions. He wants fellowship, community, the company of friends.

The way to get this fellowship isn't complicated. It's simple. Three-words simple: "I was wrong." When we blow it, that sentence is the most bold and courageous thing we can say. It's also not that hard, but many men have tricked themselves into thinking that if they acknowledge they're wrong, they'll lose their authority within the home. But really, their authority stems from them speaking the truth, even when it hurts.

DRILL: Write out the last time you felt really hurt by someone. Now, write out the last time you realized that you hurt someone. If you can do so sincerely, call that person and ask for his or her forgiveness.

When a man says he was wrong, he frees everyone else to be transparent about their weaknesses without fear of being judged. He establishes a culture of honesty, humility, and integrity. It's one of the least authoritarian and one of the most humble things a man can do, which is what makes it so critically important. As

G. K. Chesterton once put it, "When a man really tells the truth, the first truth he tells is that he himself is a liar."[3] When men begin to own up to that fact, they can radically revolutionize their homes.

THE LEAD ENCOURAGER

Guys who are more concerned for their own images and comfort only know how to be critics. They don't realize how hard things are for leaders because they don't ever step in to help. They simply stand outside, throwing their verbal grenades before walking away and letting others clean up the mess.

The family man, though, stays in the trenches and encourages those around him. He fills them with the courage they need to face the obstacles in their way. He doesn't chauvinistically insult them or abuse them, and he doesn't cowardly abdicate either. It's no encouragement to shout, "You can do it!" with your back turned while you're walking out the door. Children need the confidence that if they make mistakes it will turn out okay, so they will be willing to learn and grow into maturity. To be encouraged is to have someone help you believe that—to have someone strengthen that in you. Family men do that for those around them.

SPONGES

I'll never forget the first time I met Will. He loved to swim, run, and bike. He loved to do all three for many hours in one day. He was a rabid triathlete. Though he was in his early forties, Will could compete with guys half his age. He was also a successful businessman who had transitioned careers a decade earlier, becoming very successful in his industry.

Yet Will was failing. Sure, he was meeting the numbers in his business and nailing his times in his races. But his family was falling apart. He was trying to work sixty-plus hours a week and train twenty-plus hours a week with three elementary-age kids and a young wife. Working hard at a job you love and being passionate about a hobby are not bad things. But you are in trouble when you have a wife and little kids who feel cheated. Will ended up doing major damage to his family—but he didn't realize it until a decade later. He is on the verge of divorce and is disconnected from his kids, who learned to live without their dad.

DRILL: E-mail your closest friends with kids and offer to babysit so they can have a night off together.

It's important to have friends, but your wife must be your best friend. It's good to have a career, but your wife must be more central to you than your career. And there is nothing wrong with having a hobby, but your wife must be more important to you than your hobby.

What does that have to do with the family? Your children need to know their parents are committed to each other above every earthly relationship. When mom and dad communicate love, concern, and care for each other, children feel safe and secure. As someone once said, the most important thing a man can do for his spouse is love their children; and the most important thing a man can do for his children is to love his spouse.

ON BEING A BETTER FATHER

Start becoming a good father before you have kids. Earlier I told you I hadn't changed a diaper until I had my first child. That was a critical mistake. When my own children came, I was insecure, I had no experience, and I was no help for my wife. I made all my mistakes on my kids early on. The first four years of my daughter Glory's life, she would cry every other time I talked to her because of my voice. I have a loud, forceful tone, and I didn't know how to deploy it around children because I hadn't been around them before. If I had spent more time hanging out with other people's children, I might have been a little more prepared.

Defer to Your Wife

Here's something I just know: your wife has a sensitivity and awareness of your children that you simply do not have. She knows things about them before they do, even years before you do. Smart leaders follow others in their strengths, and it's no weakness to lean on your wife in parenting. It's simply common sense.

You Parent a Child, Not Your Children

Every child is very different. I have to argue with my son, Drew, about what he did wrong, but all I have to do is look at Glory and Grace and they wilt. My daughter Delainey requires a time-out. When we interact with our children, we interact with individuals, unique people who have their own histories, personalities, and concerns. It's easy to forget, but crucial to remember, that how we respond to one child may need to be different from how we respond to another.

Deal with Your Father Bruises

Some guys are so wounded by their dads that they unintentionally end up copying them. Other guys rebel against their fathers, so they end up being too authoritarian if their fathers were uninvolved, or they check out and let the kids run the show if they grew up beneath a dictator. In both cases, it's their own history that is setting the direction of their children's lives. Men need to work through their own issues so they don't pass them down.

Guard Your Child's Heart

You don't discipline the action; you discipline the attitude. The problem isn't simply that Drew takes Delainey's toys—it's that he is being selfish (as many of us are). And it's our job to help him see it. At the same time, when Delainey wants to help out but does something wrong, we're careful to encourage and foster her willingness while teaching her how to do it. We care more about our children's hearts right now than their deeds.

Be a Fun Dad

Be the chief enjoyer of the world. If you're always down or tired because you're working too much, you're missing out. Your family wants to play together. I didn't spend my days growing up daydreaming about having children. But now that I have kids, I spend my time thinking about the world from my children's point of view and brainstorming ways to make life interesting for them. Because you are the chief memory maker, you need to be strategic and intentional in creating an environment of playfulness and joy.

BECAUSE YOU ARE THE CHIEF MEMORY MAKER, YOU NEED TO BE STRATEGIC AND INTENTIONAL IN CREATING AN ENVIRONMENT OF PLAYFULNESS AND JOY.

EIGHT

SAY, "I LOVE YOU, MAN": THE CONNECTED MAN

CONNECTED: KNOWING AND
BEING KNOWN BY OTHER MEN

EVERY FRIDAY MORNING FOR THE PAST THIRTY YEARS,
an eclectic group of men has met for a loud and lively conversation. They talk about politics and religion, investing, and above all, the local sports scene. Some of them are very wealthy, while others are struggling to get by. But they all have their opinions and their stories and are more than happy to share them, especially if you've never visited the group before.

These guys know each other well. For years they've spoken together about their families and relationships. They aren't all on the same level of the social ladder, but they live part of their lives together and know how to connect. They are the closest thing to friends that most men will ever reach.

Most guys in their thirties, forties, and fifties simply don't have friends.[1] I asked one guy why he was so alone, and his response was blunt: "It's too hard. It's impossible to have the emotional energy and free time to work hard, provide for my family, stay connected with my wife, attend my children's activities, keep my house up, try to get to the gym, and maintain deep friendships." There simply aren't enough hours in the day. And deep friendships don't seem as important when compared to our urgent responsibilities.

Some guys struggle because they don't have anything in common with the guys they spend most of their time around. They might get along okay at work, but it's often an environment that isn't conducive to close friendships. It's hard to be friends with supervisors, and men tend to compete with peers. And it's even trickier to be friends with direct reports. The conflict of roles is hard to resolve, and introducing friendship into the mix makes it more challenging. The possibility of firing your friends or being fired by your friend is not exactly a recipe for connection.

DRILL: Call a buddy and go out to eat, play a sport, or work on a project together.

A married guy has additional challenges, including his wife's need for friendship. Two guys might get along well enough, but the wives need to connect too. Investing in a friendship at a deep level has to be a joint affair; you double date for a while, and if things don't click for everyone, you end up moving on. (And when children come along and make friends, the struggle only gets harder, as all the children have to get along too.)

In the '90s, a beer commercial lampooned the sort of bro-romance that many men think are true friendships. "I love you, man" became the catchphrase that guys would say ironically to each other, to communicate care and concern without devolving into sappiness. We don't like saying "I love you" to anyone but our wives and children, and for understandable reasons. But guys who want to be true men may need to learn how, for friendship is essential for discovering true manhood.

FRIENDSHIP AND THE UNCONNECTED MAN

From the outside, it seems that some guys have all the friends they could possibly want. They are constantly busy "hanging out" and talking sports, scotch, and ladies. And yet they still feel disconnected and isolated.

Part of the problem is that we have no idea what a friend actually is. A friend is someone who knows your hopes, dreams, and fears. They don't stay on the surface—they go deep. And they are committed to help you conquer your fears, live out your dreams, and grow in your character.

Despite people's innate need for deep friendships, 25 percent of Americans have no one to confide in.[2] It's easy to settle for friendship's counterfeits and keep relationships on the surface. These counterfeits look and smell like the real thing, but they aren't. And they come in a number of different varieties.

Acquaintances

Acquaintances are coworkers, neighbors, and the folks we cross paths with at the gym. They may know the basics about our lives and we may talk about the kids, our jobs, and the weather. We might demonstrate genuine concern for each other and listen some to each other's struggles and needs, but they don't know our hopes, dreams, and fears. They don't put themselves on the line to help us address our demons and wrestle down our insecurities. These relationships aren't fake; they simply aren't deep.

Drinking Buddies

The drinking buddy is the guy who knows your hopes, dreams, and fears, but because of his own character, he's not helping you actually realize your potential. He might take a bullet for you, but he isn't willing to challenge you to be better. He can hear you, but he can't *help* you. You aren't growing together. You have fun, you have great memories, and your families might hang out together. But your own relationship is stagnant. You're not actually becoming a better man even though you share good times.

Fans

Fans are for you as long as it helps them. Fair-weather sports fans spend money on tickets and buy memorabilia when the team is winning, but bolt when they lose. They cheer to make themselves feel better, to feel like winners. Many of us have fan friends like this. They aren't really interested in your good; they're interested in the goods they get from you.

WHAT OUR FRIENDS DO

Authentic friendship is not one-sided. It is an equal commitment from both parties. True friends both give and receive.

True friends know you and want to be known by you—celebrate you and are willing to be celebrated by you. They challenge you and seek to be challenged by you. And they serve you and are willing to be served by you.

Know and Are Known

That story you tell about the time you did that one thing? Your friends know all the points at which you embellish it. They know what the subtle shifts in your voice mean, and they recognize when your day isn't going quite right. They've heard that joke you tell more times than they can remember, but they're cool enough to recognize that everyone repeats stories. They know what you really want out of this world. They see why you do what you do. And you know all the same quirks, goals, and motivations about them too.

Celebrate and Are Celebrated

One of the most difficult challenges men face is being genuinely glad when other people succeed. We are full of envy. When others succeed, we often feel like we lose. But a friend is willing to celebrate with you, to rejoice when you rejoice. When you get a new promotion or announce a new child, they do more than simply get you drunk. They enter into your joy, making it their own.

And they are willing to let you celebrate them as well. Some guys are too proud to talk about their own accomplishments or to really celebrate their own lives, and some guys are so proud that is all they talk about. But if we don't let others into our joys, we won't let others into our sorrows. Real friends invite others into their successes and ask them to share their joy. You know you have a friend when he lets you celebrate with him.

Challenge and Are Open to Being Challenged

Friends would be easy to find if we were perfect. But we aren't. And that makes friendship difficult and sometimes painful. A friend calls out the false things you trust in, the good things that you've made the best things, the temporary things you've made the ultimate. Anyone can point out our bad behavior. It doesn't take world-class discernment to point out when we lie, display arrogance, or explode in anger. But a friend goes beneath all that with us, examining not simply our actions but our core motivations. Friends are willing not just to point out the bad fruit but to pull out the corrupt root.

MOST GUYS HAVE SURROUNDED THEMSELVES WITH FANS MASQUERADING AS FRIENDS.

A friend will focus on the sort of things we need to change. As the ancient proverb says, "Faithful are the wounds of a friend, but deceitful are the kisses of an enemy" (Prov. 27:6 NASB). The logic of this proverb is staggering. A friend who says things that feel harmful is better for us than those who are only willing to say nice things.

But most guys have surrounded themselves with fans masquerading as friends. Friends are willing to challenge because they care for a person, not because they want to hurt him. They will not merely ask how a newly divorced friend is feeling but encourage him to forgive his ex. A friend calls out the best version of a man, exposing the root of a man's struggles while instilling in him hope for the future. Friends refuse to let men live beneath their masculine privilege.

Serve and Are Served

Friends don't help men forget their burdens; they bear them. If a man gets divorced, his drinking buddies will make sure he drowns his sorrows. But they won't help him confront his own failure and forgive his ex. At best, many guys only know how to provide distracting amusements for their friends who are in pain or need help. They can only help us escape; they cannot help us thrive.

Guys actually enjoy serving each other. We are willing to load moving trucks and work on major landscaping projects together. What we don't like is *being served*. One of my neighbors recently went through a trying experience with cancer. He couldn't keep his yard up, couldn't eat much food, and couldn't do the routines of daily life. His neighbors had to step in to help him—he resisted, but couldn't say no. He told me the hardest part of having cancer wasn't the pain, the chemo, or missing work; it was the painful vulnerability of needing other people's help.

A served man is still a true man. True manhood doesn't mean we are self-sufficient or that we can control our worlds. It means recognizing our limits and acknowledging our weaknesses, which frees us to serve and be served. This is especially important for young men to realize because we will someday all grow old—and if we are going to age with honor and grace, we should start practicing our dependency now.

All the weaknesses we have in old age and when we are sick remind us of the one fundamental limitation that all men have to face: we simply cannot fix our own character. We need others to help us see our blind spots. We hurt other people, we wrong them, and we hurt ourselves. And many times we don't realize it. We simply can't fix ourselves. We are dependent on other people and dependent upon our Creator.

When it comes down to it, a friend is only a friend because he cares about something more important than the friendship itself. Friends are interested in our character more than getting along and hanging out. They are willing to know, celebrate, and serve us—even if we don't invite them. To be a friend, we must be willing to risk the friendship by speaking the hard truths and by living a life of service, even when those aren't initially welcomed. Unless we are willing to risk everything for the sake of others' good and well-being, we are not really their friends.

CULTIVATING TRUE FRIENDSHIPS

For most guys, the only true friends they have are their wives. The vast majority of guys don't even know their *own* hopes, dreams, and fears well enough to share them with someone else. But we can't get to the bottom of who we are without other people. Friends are like mirrors that help us see ourselves.

Friendship takes time to cultivate. More often than not, men don't have one or two friends. Instead, a looser group forms—a band of brothers who are all invested in a common cause or have a common interest. That doesn't mean we shouldn't open ourselves to the particular friendship of one person. But it does mean that we shouldn't be surprised if we sometimes find ourselves in groups rather than in close, one-to-one friendships.

Yet this sort of group mentality also has its dangers. Many men choose to hide there. My own temptation is to reveal part of myself to many guys, but to do so in such a way that keeps me from being accountable to change. When we are scared to be known, we are really being unwilling to grow.

In group settings it's easy to strategically reveal ourselves in a way that makes people think they're getting all of us, but they're not. We can keep the relationships entirely on our terms, only showing those parts that we are comfortable with other people knowing. True friendship, though, sees through this. Those who are real friends are able to say things about us that we don't already know and we might *never* say to anyone else.

> TO BE A FRIEND, WE MUST BE WILLING TO RISK THE FRIENDSHIP BY SPEAKING THE HARD TRUTHS.

Some guys struggle to have true friendships because they come across as needy or domineering. They assume a place of inferiority or superiority, both of which are infertile soil for friendship. The transparency that men need for friendship won't happen when others think that they'll either be sucked dry or pushed out of the way.

Friendship requires equality; you can get some of the qualities of friendship from a boss or a direct report, but the unequal power relationship will make a true friendship difficult. Friendship is a leveling force. When two men are friends, they are free to be themselves and to speak with each other without fear or hindrance. Trying to be friends with those with whom we are not equals is doomed from the start. It's like trying to date the girl who's out of your league. All you have in common is that you're upright and bipedal, and the connection can't go any deeper because of the differences.

FRIENDSHIP VERSUS CLIQUES

Most groups are rooted in affinity, especially when they first begin. Affinity groups happen when people remind us of ourselves and how great we are, magnifying our own glory. They are cliques, which create relationships by drawing a line between ourselves and other people. Those on the outside are deficient in some way, while people on the inside are not.

In his essay "The Inner Ring," C. S. Lewis explores this sort of group dynamic and people's desires to be "on the inside"— and the subtle and deadly costs that men will pay to get there.[3] We all know the phenomenon: a group forms that has its own language, its own code, its own inside jokes. We want in, but we're not. So we laugh extra loud at the jokes, we may fudge a little on what movies we have seen, and we smile and nod at stuff we don't have a clue about. We play the game so that we can get on the inside. As Lewis described it:

> In any wholesome group of people which holds together for a good purpose, the exclusions are in a sense accidental. Three or four people who are together for the sake of some piece of work exclude others because there is work only for so many or because the others can't in fact do it. Your little musical

group limits its numbers because the rooms they meet in are only so big. But your genuine Inner Ring exists for exclusion. There'd be no fun if there were no outsiders. The invisible line would have no meaning unless most people were on the wrong side of it. Exclusion is no accident; it is the essence.[4]

Friendship, on the other hand, is expansive and rejoices in people's differences. It welcomes new people into its midst because it understands that people are enhanced, rather than diminished, by new relationships. It isn't a clique; it's a community.

It was C. S. Lewis again who knew this best. In his book *The Four Loves*, Lewis described his expectation that his relationship with a close friend—writer J. R. R. Tolkien—would improve when their mutual friend died. But he finds out the opposite is true. He put it:

> In each of my friends there is something that only some other friend can fully bring out. By myself I am not large enough to call the whole man into activity; I want other lights than my own to show all his facets. Now that Charles is dead, I shall never again see Ronald's reaction to a specifically Caroline joke. Far from having more of Ronald, having him "to myself" now that Charles is away, I have less of Ronald . . . We possess each friend not less but more as the number of those with whom we share him increases.[5]

Personally, when I left for college, I was sick of guys who were like me. Rather than go hang out with a bunch of jocks, I made friends with guys who were different from me and who were strong where I was weak. I intentionally tried to invite different types of people into my life. And by making friends with different types of guys, I expanded my world.

Guys who only hang out in an inner ring of friends eventually quit growing. They will only add new members if they can get something from them and if they conform to the preexisting standards of the group. And the stagnating social relationships will lead to a stagnating soul.

FRIENDSHIP ON THE WAY

It's been said that women are face-to-face, but men are shoulder to shoulder. In other words, women connect with each other while men connect accomplishing something.[6] Guys like *doing things*. Friendships are forged in the trenches, in the struggle to accomplish something.

> FRIENDSHIPS ARE FORGED IN THE TRENCHES, IN THE STRUGGLE TO ACCOMPLISH SOMETHING.

When we love the work we're doing, for instance, we see how valuable and helpful others are to it getting done. We'll learn to be grateful for their contributions and their perspective. And we'll get to know them as we see them struggle, learn, and grow on their way toward our destination.

Geek out with me for a second. Sam and Frodo in the *Lord of the Rings* are a classic example of friends. They fight for each other, care deeply about each other, and even fight *with* each other. It's not a smooth road they travel, but they travel it together. Despite their struggles, they end up committed to each other's good and well-being. And their common cause, their mission, joins them together in ways they never knew were possible when they set out.

In a sense, friendship is forged most when two guys look outward and discern how best they can serve the world shoulder to shoulder. It's forged when they cultivate a mission and then live it out.

THE PRACTICES OF FRIENDSHIP

Friendship doesn't just happen. Instead, there are several practices that help men cultivate friendships with other guys.

Presence

Men need to gather together routinely. I meet with a group of guys once a week. We gather before we go to work and talk to each other and pray for each other between sips of coffee. We sacrifice a little of our sleep because we know how important it is for us to spend time together.

That's the routine dimension. But it's also helpful to get away together, as friends, and go on retreats. The relationships forged in those concentrated times can be very deep. And old relationships, college relationships, can be renewed and strengthened very easily in those times as well. It doesn't take long to go deep with someone you've known for a long time.

For a lot of guys, presence can simply mean making ourselves available to other people and allowing others to enter into our daily rhythms. When I work in my yard, I routinely get into conversations with my neighbor. And when I run errands, I invite young leaders in our organization along with me. It's odd, but it also allows us time together while doing the mundane activities of life. Friendship is often found within the ordinary.

Productivity

There's something real to a friendship where you're producing something together. Real friends have a cause; something deeper than just themselves brings them together.

But friendship is also productive in the sense that it builds character in one another. Hard words from a friend can be like the pruning that goes on in gardening: a rose emerges, but only after a lot of the plant has been cut off in winter. A real friendship isn't simply oriented toward having a good time together, or even hearing each other's opinions about barbecue and baseball. It is oriented toward the formation of virtue in the other person and pursues such formation intentionally.

Perseverance

Sometimes people drift away, but a lot of times a crisis or disagreement drives them away. Friendship doesn't mean gathering with guys we always get along with; it means learning to get along with the guys we gather with. It takes perseverance to face hard conversations, poverty and wealth, good times and bad. A good friendship resembles a good marriage in this way. Perseverance means fighting through each other's failures— the hurts, the brokenness—and enduring the wounds in order to cultivate a relationship.

Making real friends isn't easy. It's an investment, though, that pays rewards in ways we could never imagine. The more we are willing to treasure and cultivate friendships, the less attached we will be to the possessions, status, and power many men think will make them happy. Our lives will be full of the goodness and joy that comes from working shoulder to shoulder with those who care about us, and whom we care about. And all the petty and temporary concerns we face will slowly be crowded out, leaving only the joyful sacrificial living of true manhood.

FRIENDSHIP DOESN'T MEAN GATHERING WITH GUYS WE ALWAYS GET ALONG WITH; IT MEANS LEARNING TO GET ALONG WITH THE GUYS WE GATHER WITH.

NINE

FEEL SOMETHING WITHOUT CRYING AT EVERYTHING: THE EMOTIONAL MAN

EMOTIONAL: ACCESSING A FULL
RANGE OF EMOTIONS WITHOUT BEING
DOMINATED BY ANY OF THEM

WE ALL KNOW THE TYPE: TOUGH AS NAILS, A NON-CRIER, a man who isn't afraid of anything. He is a man's man who always gets the girl while never acting like one. He is immovable, like a rock. But like a rock, everything is hard, including his heart.

This guy was the most interesting man in the world, before the beer commercial. He used to be the template exemplified in

John Wayne—tough, unemotional, and in control. The ideal tough guy is being resurrected in the marketing campaigns for Old Spice and Dos Equis, which are pitching a retro version of unemotional manhood.

The idea that men don't cry is dead. Some men are the softer, sensitive sort who push their wives and girlfriends to watch *The Notebook* and even supply the Kleenex. Politicians and sports coaches these days are frequently seen shedding tears when things go their way—or when they don't. One study in England found that 90 percent of the surveyed respondents thought it had become more acceptable for men to cry over the past twenty years.[1]

Men have emotions, but many of us don't know what to do with them. We fear our emotions more than a receding hairline. We have few models of affectionate men who are still strong, men who feel things deeply without allowing their emotions to determine how they live. Put simply, we have zero vision for how to be emotionally healthy.[2]

That's the conclusion of Audrey Nelson, a communications expert who has studied the differences between men and women extensively. As she puts it:

> In an analysis of 500,000 adults, men rated just as high as women in emotional awareness. But men process and express emotions differently than women, and they have no roadmap for how to combine the masculine requirement of being strong and emotional at the same time. A woman cries and a man loses his temper; that seems to be the pervasive theme in many conflicts. Men and women react differently; she shows her vulnerability and he must remain in control.[3]

In the mid-twentieth century, C. S. Lewis described what he called, in the title of one book, *The Abolition of Man*. Lewis argued that the education system had stopped caring for people's emotions, and as a result people either didn't have the sort of emotional life they were made for, or they didn't know what to do with their emotions. Men (and women), he argued, don't have a sense of the "spirited element"—which he locates in the chest—that moves us to action in the right situation. Spiritedness stands between our desires and our thoughts, between our lusts and our reasons, between our bellies and our heads. Instead of deep wells of healthy emotional energy, Lewis suggested, we have been made barren and empty, what he calls "men without chests."[4] Spiritedness has been educated out of us as the narratives and memories of heroes from the past have been forgotten.

There are two options for men who lack chests. Some men let their stomachs rule them. They end up pursuing nothing except sex, comfort, advancement, or riches. They don't have to assert themselves because they frequently do whatever they want.

Other men let their heads rule them. Rather than giving in to selfish desires, their lives become one long three-step plan to self-improvement. They read all the self-help books and create life plans, sometimes in an effort not to have to deal with "distracting" emotions. They want order in and for their lives, and they'll cut themselves off from their deepest passions to pursue it.

The man in the middle is the affectionate man, the man who allows himself to feel deeply about the world but is also interested in feeling appropriately. He's not dominated by his emotions, but he doesn't suppress them either.

Consider a feeling like anger. Men who are dominated by anger are often chauvinistic, manipulative, and abusive. They want to control the world because they can't control themselves. They feel mad, they don't know why, and they don't know what to do with it. So they lash out and endanger everyone else around them.

At the same time, a man who suppresses his anger ends up disconnecting himself from his heart. Some guys are in control, and that is the problem. The full range of emotional responses—warmth, tenderness, affection, grief, joy—are neutered, which keeps them from really engaging others from their hearts.

RELATIONSHIPS AND HAPPINESS

For the past seventy years, researchers at Harvard University have followed the lives of 268 men. Called the Grant Study, this project offers unique insights into the ways in which men understand their own lives and existence.

In an article summarizing some of the results of the study, *New York Times* columnist David Brooks argued that developing the capacity for intimacy in childhood made a massive difference in the rest of their lives:

> Having a warm childhood was powerful. As George Vaillant, the study director, sums it up in "Triumphs of Experience," his most recent summary of the research, "It was the capacity for intimate relationships that predicted flourishing in all aspects of these men's lives.
>
> Of the 31 men in the study incapable of establishing

intimate bonds, only four are still alive. Of those who were better at forming relationships, more than a third are living . . . In case after case, the magic formula is capacity for intimacy combined with persistence, discipline, order and dependability. The men who could be affectionate about people and organized about things had very enjoyable lives.[5]

Emotional health isn't the enemy of true manhood. It's the secret to it. Men who are raised in households that are warm, affectionate, and caring are often more equipped to be strong, courageous, and bold in healthy ways because they know who they are, and they know they are loved. They know they don't have to prove themselves in order to be accepted, which grounds their masculine identities.

Men typically don't know what to do with anger or fear, and some men even struggle with joy or gratitude. Many men don't know what to do when they are really happy any more than they know what to do when they are really sad. They don't know how to take a compliment any more than they know how to take a complaint.

In a long article summarizing a study by George Vaillant that followed a number of men for their whole lives, Joshua Wolf Shenk points out that men struggle with positive emotions as much as they do negative ones, as positive emotions make men "more vulnerable." He tells a story about one doctor whose patients wrote thank-you cards at the end of his career, which he promptly stowed away in a box.

Eight years later, Vaillant interviewed the man, who proudly pulled the box down from his shelf. "George, I don't know what you're going to make of this," the man said, as he began to cry, "but I've never read it." "It's very hard," Vaillant said, "for most of us to tolerate being loved."[6]

Look at that last sentence again. "It's very hard for most of us to tolerate being loved." That's an astonishing summation of how many guys think about themselves. Men don't know how to allow others to praise them because they are either afraid they won't feel gratitude or they don't know how to feel gratitude.

Sometimes it's not the strength of a man's emotions that scares him—it's the mystery of his emotions. We don't just need more emotions; we need emotions in the right place at the right time.

Depression	ANGER	Passion
Rage Control Anxiety	FEAR	Faith
Resentment	HURT	Healing Courage
Self-Pity	SAD	Acceptance (ok w/ what is not ok)
Apathy	LONELY	Intimacy
Toxic shame	GUILT	Forgiveness Freedom
Toxic shame	SHAME	Humility
Sensuous/sensual experience w/o heart	GLAD	Joy (w/sadness)

Feelings Chart © Dr. Chip Dodd *The Voice of the Heart: A Call to Full Living*

Jeff Schulte of the Sage Hill Institute suggests there are eight core emotions, and that these emotions either become virtues in men or they are debased and take men away from virtue. Many men allow their feeling of hurt to sour into resentment, rather than seeking healing and cultivating the courage to face their pain. Other men let their anger rot into depression, instead of letting it deepen their passion for justice. He includes this chart, with the problematic emotion on the left and the goal on the right.

The goal of true manhood isn't being stoic and never feeling any pain. True men take their emotions and reform them. True men's emotions don't destroy them or the people they love; they are fuel for true virtue.

WHEN MEN ACT UP
(OR DON'T ACT AT ALL)

A good friend had planned an entire weekend away with his wife. Finally, it would be just the two of them—a weekend to relax, reconnect, and rekindle a romance that had grown cold. All the pieces were in place: a nice bed-and-breakfast, an itinerary with nothing on it, and chocolate.

Then the wheels fell off.

As often happens when there hasn't been any real conversation in a long time, issues that were lurking bubbled out because of an errant word. The weekend dissolved into tears, anger, frustration, and more tears as months of buildup came to a boiling point. Rather than returning from the weekend renewed and refreshed, the man came away uncertain and angry, disappointed because his plan for connecting with his wife was thwarted.

But rather than address and acknowledge his disappointment in a healthy way with his wife, the man buried it. He told himself he was really okay and justified settling into a cool distance because life was so busy. He didn't stay engaged with his wife; he withdrew and refused to allow her into what he was feeling. Rather than voicing his emotions and allowing his wife to enter into them, even though it would have been hard, he began acting out, pouring himself into pornography to placate his desire for a real connection with his wife.

DRILL: Emotions often come to the surface when we are alone. Go spend an hour sitting in silence and pay careful attention to what comes before your mind. Do you feel angry, sad, or nothing at all?

Men are like an old car with engine troubles when it comes to emotions. Oil, antifreeze, and transmission fluids leak out slowly—or worse, all at once! Emotions are the same way. If we don't keep them up, if we don't acknowledge them and talk about them, then they'll leak out in our snarky side comments or our passive-aggressive swipes at our friends, spouses, or kids. Or we'll just blow up, putting those around us in danger and creating an environment of fear and uncertainty.

THE HEART OF SPORTS

I love sports. I have been a St. Louis Cardinals fan my entire life. I get excited every time the Cardinals make it to the World

Series, which thankfully has been pretty often in my lifetime. I use sports in my writing and my teaching because it's a subject I know and love and that other guys do too.

But I don't want to talk about sports just because I don't know how to talk about anything else. And I don't *ever* want to be more excited about sports than I am about my children, my wife, my work, or my friends. I want my love for sports to bleed into my priorities, to enhance them and not minimize them.

But amazingly, not everyone is that way. One report from Britain suggested that 10 percent of their men said a win by England in the Euro 2012 cup (some soccer tournament—I have no idea what that is) would mean more than *their wedding day*.[7] That's how many reported it, anyway. Who knows how many of them were actually willing to consider the question before finally deciding in favor of their weddings?

There's something revealing about all that emotional intensity. You can see it when guys get into a game they're playing or watching, when they're all rooting for the same team. Men connect emotionally. They will weep and celebrate together there like nowhere else. They will be more open with one another, more honest and truthful, because they care about something together.

Guys are okay sharing their emotions when they are totally invested in something and when they are in a world they know and can navigate. For many men, sports are comfortable and understandable, and so men are safe to show their emotions. Passion is expected, and tears are acceptable on the field or court. For some men, the time they spend playing or watching sports is the only time they really feel alive.

Additionally, men are free to express emotions in the realm of sports because there are cultural rituals that help guide them. Conversely, there are few rituals for men in other realms and fewer models of emotionally healthy men. This is why many of us just don't know when and where we're supposed to stay composed and when it's okay to go to pieces. It is also why men tend to limit themselves to showing emotions only at weddings and childbirth. We know what we can and can't do there. Everywhere else? No idea.

> WHEN MEN OPEN UP AND TELL THEIR FAMILIES AND FRIENDS THEIR HOPES, DREAMS, AND FEARS, THEY CREATE AN ENVIRONMENT OF SAFETY AND SECURITY.

Here is the truth. When men open up and tell their families and friends their hopes, dreams, and fears, they create an environment of safety and security. When others around us don't know what we are feeling, they will be uncertain and hesitant toward us. Those close to us want to know us. Such knowledge is necessary if they are going to meaningfully contribute to our well-being, and vice versa. Otherwise, they're going to feel as alienated and disconnected from us as we are from our emotions.

What's more, when we invite others into our lives by sharing our emotions with them, we strengthen their ability to be emotionally vulnerable and transparent with us. Emotional bonds go both directions. As we take the first step and define and describe our feelings, we create space for others to do the same.

WHAT TO DO WITH EMOTIONS

Some of our emotions seem too powerful for us. Take anger, for instance. Many of us have real and genuine anger issues that we need help with. A few are physically abusive with those close to them. Other guys inflict verbal abuse on others. They can't control their tongues, and so they let them run with sarcastic insults, biting words, and denigrating put-downs. If physical or verbal abuse is a pattern for you, this is your wake-up call to meet with a counselor ASAP.

But most of us probably aren't abusing others. We just have moments of anger, frustration, or disappointment that cause us to lash out.

So what can you do with anger?

The old rule of counting to ten when we are angry actually has some merit to it. We might need to feel our destructive emotions even if we don't necessarily invite others into them at that moment the way we might with joy or gratitude or happiness. We may need to slip away, be by ourselves, and reflect about the reasons for our anger or frustration and examine whether we are ourselves culpable for them.

That sort of process is similar to what a counselor will do, and some of us probably need to go there in order to get help to reach down to the root issues. But in the meantime, it's not bad to be "slow to anger," as the Bible says. And if we find that we are quick to anger, we should slow everything else in our lives down by giving ourselves more space so that when the anger begins to arise, we have room to deal with it well.

Similarly, men can develop the ability to watch and mirror

other people's healthy emotions. By inviting others to share what they are feeling and entering into their joy and sorrow, men develop the virtue of empathy. We weep with those who weep and laugh with those who laugh.

Empathy isn't often talked about, but it's important for healthy relationships with other people. When men don't have it, we will lack the ability to genuinely connect with others at the deepest levels. Empathy is a sort of meaningful listening. When men empathize with others, we work to understand what they are going through and to see things from their perspective. We may not be able to fix things, as many of us will be tempted to do, but if we work on simply feeling what others are feeling, we'll see our own ability to feel deeply and appropriately expanded.

THE TOUGH AND TENDER MAN

Men need to be more attuned to their emotions. But contrary to the stereotype, that doesn't mean they need to become "soft." In fact, the more aware of our emotions we become, and the more empathy we build, the more courage and strength we will have to fight against evil. It's not just the ability to connect with our spouses, friends, or children that we lose if we disconnect from our emotions. It's our ability to be courageous, to speak boldly, to passionately strive for justice and goodness.

Take my friend Josh, who is one of the most passionate guys I know. He is deeply emotional with his family and friends; he cares about them more than he has words to express. But he is also working tirelessly within our city to provide jobs for those who need them, redevelop neighborhoods that have eroded due to neglect, and reinforce existing social support networks among low-income communities. He's a fierce warrior against injustice and racism, but he's also the sort of guy who tries to make everyone around him feel safe and warm. He's tender and tough at the same time.

That sort of fusion of toughness and tenderness is rare. We have a difficult time finding the right balance in part because most of us have never seen it. We all know the guy who could break you apart with his hands, but we don't know the guy with that sort of power who also makes everyone feel warm and protected. We know the guy who wants everyone to share their emotions and who will weep at the drop of a hat. But we don't know the guy who feels things deeper than everyone else but is also able to go to war when his family is threatened.

Toughness and tenderness aren't opposites. They belong together in a man. True manhood takes both the strength to stand up against injustice and the softness to hold our children when they're scared. True manhood requires cultivating the passionate courage to protect those who are endangered and the sensitivity to allow our wives to pour out all their deepest yearnings to us. We need men who have both the tenderness to cry with those who are suffering and the toughness to tell those who are doing wrong to stop.

> TOUGHNESS AND TENDERNESS AREN'T OPPOSITES. THEY BELONG TOGETHER IN A MAN.

True manliness is tough without being dominating. It is tender without being weak. We don't need to cut off our emotions or let them control us. We don't need to turn into John

Wayne or the blubbering guys who cry at everything. Our emotions can move us to love others and fight for the good. They can help our relationships rather than harm them. They can help us become true men and good men rather than men who are laughed at or feared.

TEN

FIND THE RIGHT ARENA: THE FIGHTING MAN

FIGHTING: THE WILLINGNESS TO ENGAGE IN CONFLICT FOR THE COMMON GOOD

STEVE JOBS BEGAN A TECHNOLOGICAL REVOLUTION THAT is still happening today. Apple became the world's leading tech company because Jobs was hyperfocused on making products that no one had dreamed of and that everyone would want. He was relentless, refusing to compromise his principles or his vision in making Apple the most innovative company in the world.

But he also paid a steep price. Had Jobs been allowed complete control, the very things that made him great would have destroyed the company. His obsessive, meticulous approach to products might have prevented any of them from ever actually being shipped. He fought relentlessly to build beautiful products, but his family and personal relationships suffered. He built an empire but lost what matters the most.[1]

The sort of excellence Jobs demanded doesn't happen naturally; he had to fight hard for it. He approached his work with a winner-take-all mentality, like an ancient gladiator might have. He fought against the resistance and inertia that breed mediocrity. He was a warrior.

Business isn't the wrong arena to fight in, but it isn't the only arena. It was, however, the only arena for Jobs. Everything else served it. His family and personal relationships all took a backseat to the work he was doing.

Many of us are like Jobs. For some, the only arena we really care to fight in is our football teams. We will do whatever it takes to defend our favorite team or win our fantasy football league. For others, it's politics. Every question is a war, and the only thing that matters is the other team losing. Some guys make the world revolve around their kids. As long as they are okay, nothing else matters.

Getting our lives right in those spheres is important. But the main battle we face isn't in the arenas we enter; the core battle is within, with ourselves. Our character is good that is greater than a corporate empire, or a life full of fun weekends, or children who make the honor roll. Without good character, everything else is meaningless. If a man's character is rotten, then with enough time it will eventually spoil the rest of his life.

Character is the essence of a man. It is the soil from which the fruit of our lives springs. Our character is made up of our motivations, thoughts, and behaviors. It is who we are when no one is looking. Our character is an atmosphere that pervades every part of our lives. It shapes how we go about our work, our families, our hobbies, and our play. It is the inner core that determines what sort of legacy we will leave behind.

Good character does not simply arrive on its own. Parents discipline children while modeling good character because they know it doesn't happen naturally. As we grow up, we see more clearly how difficult good character is to win. But striving for good character is the one battle that will always be worth fighting.

> CHARACTER IS THE ESSENCE OF A MAN. IT IS THE SOIL FROM WHICH THE FRUIT OF OUR LIVES SPRINGS.

Men are fighters. From the junior high locker room to the frat party rumble to the Octagon, many men love to see a good fight.[2] There is something in us that is drawn to seeing who is the strongest, the toughest, the one who can take a punch. There is a real sense that this is part of what it means to be a man. Men are made to compete, made to battle, wired to fight.

But men are made for more than throwing hands with other men. The greatest enemy men face is themselves. The true battle men must fight requires cultivating the courage, integrity, and self-sacrificial giving that has marked the great men of the past.

THE MEANING OF CHARACTER

Good character is hard to achieve because it requires looking at our weaknesses and addressing them accordingly. It is one thing for a man to acknowledge that he has told a lie. It is another to acknowledge that lying is habitual and he is a *liar*. It is hard to look closely at the mirror.

The most pressing danger men face is not their failures but their triumphs, not their stumbles but their successes. A little success is a dangerous thing to a man. We don't have to ask questions about our character as long as we are feeling successful. Similarly, we can avoid questions about the costs of our success and whether the end justifies the means. Men often use success to paper over a hollow center and to shut down hard questions about themselves.

One of the most humbling things we can do is to face up to the reality that *we* are the problem—and it is also one of the central steps every man must take to enter true manhood. For me, that has meant facing the fact that my gifts and energy have helped the organizations that I lead to grow, but my pride in those gifts and my workaholism have also harmed many people under my care and hindered our organizational progress.

Some guys tell themselves that who they are on their best days represents their true character, much like the guy who has a great round of golf and announces he should be on the PGA tour. Just because you have a few good holes doesn't make you a great golfer.

Others redirect attention from their character to the areas where they experience success, justifying failures on grounds that they're doing all right elsewhere. They redefine the fight by changing the arenas. When our wives press us about how we need to spend time with our children, we point to our war at work to justify our absence at home. If we are failing in our work, we point to the struggles we have in our home life. And if we get a little success in one area, then we use it to excuse slacking in others.

Part of our problem is that we don't want to do the work to

find the root of our struggles. We'd rather stay on the surface, where things are clear and comfortable. Our tendency is to turn away from seeing things in us as habits and toward rationalizing and justifying ourselves and our lives.

Some of us are also ignorant that the fight is going on and we do everything we can to keep out the hints that all is not well. We surround ourselves with enablers, people who are more interested in our material and external success than whether we are becoming better men. Or we bring a knife to a gunfight, thinking the struggle for character was nothing more challenging than an afternoon nap.

THE FOES WE FACE

Imagine your perfect life for a second—the sort of life you've always wanted. What does it look like? How do you spend your time? What sort of atmosphere pervades it? What thoughts dominate your brain? You can tell a man's vision for his ideal life by how he spends his downtime and what he thinks about when his mind is free.

In my experience and research, there are four different sources that drive men—distinct motivations that organize and catalyze much of our behavior. Most of the time, these internal drives are like the iceberg beneath the surface. They can only be discerned through our actions, yet they are powerful and frequently destructive.[3]

> YOU CAN TELL A MAN'S VISION FOR HIS IDEAL LIFE BY HOW HE SPENDS HIS DOWNTIME AND WHAT HE THINKS ABOUT WHEN HIS MIND IS FREE.

To show how this works, I want to use an example that all men deal with: money. Some of us enjoy investing and the meticulous nature of budgeting and cost-benefit analysis. Others outsource money stuff to their wives or their financial planners. Whether you are a "money guy" or not, the example of money will help us address character deficiencies.

Motivation I: Comfort

"Life only has meaning—I only have worth—if I have this pleasure and a particular standard of life."

What we seek: comfort (privacy, lack of stress, independence)
Price we are willing to pay: reduced productivity
Greatest nightmare: stress, demands
Others often feel: hurt, neglected
Problem emotion: boredom

The thing that makes vacations so good is that we are able to pursue what gives us peace and doesn't have anything to do with the cares of this world. We were made to enjoy environments where we can relax and detox from the pressures of life. The problem with a person who is compelled by comfort is that he lives life as if it were one big vacation.

When it comes to money, men motivated primarily from comfort earn and spend money to insulate themselves from the frustrations of others and rigors of daily life. They avoid boredom at all costs, so they continually purchase new gadgets and toys and invest in their hobbies and other distractions. Those who pursue comfort see others, even those closest to them, as potential obstacles to their own satisfaction, because people make demands upon them. As a result, men motivated by comfort only invest in others if their low-maintenance, hassle-free life is adequately insulated.

Motivation 2: Approval

"Life only has meaning—I only have worth—if I am loved and respected by the people whose opinion I value most."

What we seek: affirmation, love, relationship
Price we are willing to pay: less independence
Greatest nightmare: rejection
Others often feel: smothered
Problem emotion: cowardice

We were all created with a desire to be loved. This desire is healthy and natural. There is nothing better than being with people we know approve of us and are truly for us. The problem for the person who is driven by approval is that he lives for and demands the affirmation of others.

People motivated by approval will do just about anything to make a loved one happy, including spending excessively to buy the acceptance of others. They may use their earning potential to make others proud of their accomplishments. Approval addicts tend to overcommit, overpromise, and overstate in order to gain affirmation. They are radically insecure and fear rejection more than harming their character. Often, those closest to someone who cares most deeply about approval feel smothered by his neediness, as his desire to be loved cannot realistically be met by any human being.

Motivation 3: Control

"Life only has meaning—I only have worth—if I am able to get mastery over my life."

What we seek: control (self-discipline, certainty, standards)
Price we are willing to pay: loneliness, lack of spontaneity
Greatest nightmare: uncertainty
Others often feel: condemned
Problem emotion: worry

Men want to do everything they can to ensure that circumstances and situations turn out the way they should, that they "deliver the goods." The desire to carry a task from idea to implementation helps men lead well. Those who are driven by control, however, are often obsessed with making things go exactly as they planned, and often pay for it through deep-seated anxiety and worry. The mantra of a true control freak is, "If I want it done right, I have to do it myself," which also communicates to others, "It's my way or the highway."

Control freaks typically know where every penny goes, and they often self-righteously look down their noses at those who appear less on top of their finances. Wealthy or poor, control produces worrisome questions like, "Will I make enough?" or, "Am I saving enough?" The marks of pursuing control most obviously surface when change or unexpected events, like economic recessions, threaten the illusion that they can manage everything.

Motivation 4: Power

"Life only has meaning—I only have worth—if I have power and influence over others."

What we seek: power (success, winning, influence)
Price we are willing to pay: burdens, responsibility
Greatest nightmare: humiliation
Others often feel: used
Problem emotion: anger

People motivated by power love to compete. They tend to excel in sports, business, and whatever else in which they participate. And while competition is a good thing, the man motivated by power can't live without it, leaving the people around him feeling used and beaten. In regard to money, the person driven by power may be driven to risky things, like gambling or short-term moneymaking schemes. Or he may just want his business to win, not only crushing the competition but also those who work with him and under him.

Another way to describe the power guy, however, is to say that his primary motivation in life is not so much to win as to avoid losing. All is well with people who pursue power as long as they are winning. But losing exposes their deep insecurity. Losing brings anger, which can be accompanied by verbal or even physical abuse. Losing can bring hatred of the self and disdain for those who "cost" them the victory. Those close to power-lovers often feel used, undervalued, and exhausted from the up-and-down cycle of winning and losing.

DRILL: Ask the three closest people in your life what they think is your primary motivation. Don't say anything in response or be defensive. Just listen and receive what they have to say.

———

We operate out of these source motivations all the time. They come out in ways we haven't been able to identify even in the charts on the preceding pages. They show themselves in our dreams, hopes, anger, and disappointment about the world. Those sorts of problems, the issues that get us into trouble on a day-to-day basis, are often just the surface problems. Beneath them, we have the wrong vision for our lives. We are building on the wrong foundation.

For a lot of us, on the surface it might seem as though we're doing okay. We spend time with our families, we pay the bills, and we don't lie or cheat at work. But if we are doing all those things for the wrong reasons, then we're not really that much better off. When it comes to being a man, we need to reach the point where we don't simply do the right things but we do them for the right reasons.

Power, control, approval, and comfort are all *good* things. When we have them in the right balance and pursue them for the right reasons, they're important to our sense of well-being.

Personally, I have been motivated by power for as long as I can remember. It didn't matter much what I was doing; I was going to come out on top, one way or the other. In some cases, that meant bending all the rules. I remember looking around at my friends who were struggling to pay bills and realizing that I could work a ton and make not much money, or I could sell steroids instead. Because I wanted it all, I took the riskier but more lucrative route.

The upside of my motivation is that I can often find talented people and let them do what they're good at without bothering them. As long as they're succeeding, I don't need to see them. The downside is that once things get up and going, I get bored and then move on. As a friend once said of me, I'm like the kid who builds an awesome fort and brings his friends over . . . and then goes and builds a new fort. Because I want power, I struggle to develop others, which often leaves them feeling used and bitter. I don't want to be this way—and through God's grace, I'm learning that I don't have to be this way. But overcoming my thirst for power is a war that I simply can't fight alone.

When we allow our source motivations to dominate us, we end up destroying our relationships with the people around us. I tend to give my children a lot of space to explore, a lot of freedom to enjoy the world around them. But the danger is that by giving them lots of independence they don't get to enjoy me as well. When people around us are a means to our own comfort, our sense of affirmation and security, our own sense of power or control, then they simply become stepping-stones on the way toward our ideal lives. And when we get there, we won't need them anymore.

One of the major themes of this book has been that a lot of our deepest struggles are influenced by our relationships—or lack thereof—with our fathers. Beneath my own struggles is a hunger to be validated by my father. Even though my dad was imperfect, he really was my hero in a lot of ways. His absence from my life drove me to "succeed." I wanted to win, to do better at everything, because I tricked myself into believing that if I did so, my father would be proud.

Those motivations are so interwoven into our characters and histories that we are powerless to transform them on our own. We have been living out of them and reinforcing them our entire lives, and they are so much a part of us that even if we could step back all the way and see them, we wouldn't know where to begin to change. Character is like an onion: our pursuit of power plays out on the surface of our decisions, but if we peel back that layer, there's simply more of the same. Our thoughts, emotions, dreams, fears, and behavior are all shaped by our fundamental motivation. Only, in our case, the core is rotten. Until, that is, we can figure out how to satisfy our deep and insatiable desire for our fathers' acceptance.

The good news is that it can be satisfied. There was a man a few thousand years back who happened to be a misfit. His brothers didn't trust him, he was smart enough to be teaching at age twelve, and his parents didn't understand him. He simply didn't fit in anywhere.

Yet the moment things changed for him—the moment his skills and abilities were unleashed—was the moment a voice came out of the heavens and affirmed him unconditionally. The man was, of course, Jesus, and the voice was from his Father in heaven. "This is my beloved Son," the voice said, "in whom I am well pleased" (Matt. 3:17). Only, Jesus hadn't really done much of anything yet except work as a carpenter. Yet he would go on to have a life that revolutionized history—that altered every-thing, even for those who never believe in him.

Jesus was able to face death as an innocent man because he had heard the voice of his Father welcoming him. He knew what his gifts were, but he needed them to be released. He needed to be called out in order to be turned loose.

There will be no end to our striving, no conclusion to our pursuit to peel back the layers of the onion to find the magical fix for ourselves. The only way forward is to confess our faults and our shortcomings and to acknowledge the brokenness of our core motivations and our impotence before them. Only then can we begin to pursue the life of the heroic man and be transformed by Jesus, who was the hero on our behalf.

ELEVEN

GET WHAT YOU WANT: THE HEROIC MAN

HEROIC: A DEATH-DEFYING, SACRIFICIAL AFFIRMATION OF ANOTHER'S GOOD ABOVE OUR OWN

QUENTIN TARANTINO IS A MASTER OF HIS CRAFT. HIS movies are as violent and gritty as any that have been made, but the violence is never senseless. He's a smart guy and his movies are more savvy than they might appear.

His films fascinate me because the heroes are rarely who we expect them to be. In *Pulp Fiction*, the film that put Tarantino on the map, Bruce Willis's character functions as a sort of hero. He kills the other boxer in a fight that he had been paid to lose. He saves Marsellus Wallace from being raped by a cop. In *Inglourious Basterds*, the German who is affectionately called "the Jew Hunter" is the person most responsible for winning the war. A consistent theme of Tarantino's movies is that the hero is the person we would never choose.

Despite all the violence, Tarantino's films often capture profound moments of dialogue. In *Kill Bill 2*, the head of a league of assassins, Bill, philosophizes with a former protégé who is trying to kill him to get revenge for taking her daughter and nearly killing her on her wedding day. The topic: superheroes and Superman.

"Clark Kent is Superman's critique on the whole human race," Bill says.[1] Most superheroes, like Batman and Spiderman, weren't born that way, Bill explains. But Superman is who he is. He doesn't have an alter ego that's a superhero. He *is* a different race altogether, and his alter ego is the weak, cowardly, and bumbling Clark Kent. Judging by Superman's choice, he doesn't exactly have a high view of humans.

WE HAVE BEEN MADE TO BE HEROES—TO SACRIFICE OURSELVES FOR OTHERS AND TO BE UNRELENTING IN OUR PURSUIT OF GOODNESS, JUSTICE, AND THE TRUTH.

I used to believe that everyone wanted to be a hero, that given the right opportunity, every man would rise to the challenge. But we don't all want to be heroes. Some of us would rather be Clark Kent, eager to slink away at the sight of trouble and to run from the presence of danger. We'd rather hang out, watching movies about superheroes, than trying to be one.

There may not be an *S* on your chest, but there is a mark on your soul. We have been made to be heroes—to sacrifice ourselves for others and to be unrelenting in our pursuit of goodness, justice, and the truth. There's something deep within us that takes us back to when we were little boys, dreaming of glorious acts of courage in the fight between good and evil.

FORMS OF PRIDE

Men have lots of pride. They know who they are; they know what they want, and they go after it. Pride isn't necessarily a bad thing. When a child does something well, the first thing he does is run and tell his parents. He is proud of his work, and he may have reasons to be.

But most of the time, rather than pointing to our work, pride points to ourselves. Such pride distorts and destroys us. It is a deadly poison that leaves no part of our lives safe. Pride twists our understanding of heroism so that we either avoid becoming true heroes or believe we can become heroes on our own. At its core, pride is worship of the unholy trinity of me, myself, and I. Pride is undue focus on the self and what we can and cannot do on our own.

Pride gets expressed in lots of ways. In fact, its flexibility is one of the things that makes it so difficult to root out. It's the nature of pride to hide itself from us, even if other people can discern it in us and we can see it in others. The man who is proud rarely thinks of himself as proud. He may think of himself as competitive, domineering, or lazy. But beneath those is often a sense of self-aggrandizement—a glorification of ourselves.

One of the main ways men project their pride is through self-pity. Men with this kind of pride see their lives as perpetually too hard and their schedules too busy, and they feel as though bad breaks happen to them too often. They are so focused on their constant suffering and their endless struggles that they have no room—emotional or otherwise—to help anyone else. This kind of pride causes a man to be permanently fixated on the rearview mirror; his life becomes a whirlwind of regrets, missed opportunities, and unrealized potential. This kind of pride flows from the unhealed wounds of the past.

Others show pride in their self-protectiveness, which prevents men from entering into any situation if there is the slightest hint of risk. They've built up their defenses and have protected themselves so well that they are virtually impenetrable to everyone. They fear being disappointed by people, so they don't engage with them. They don't expect much so they don't experience much. They don't want to let others in because they think they don't need them or they are worried about being exposed. This type of pride is the result of being hurt and betrayed by those whom they once trusted.

These two forms of pride keep men on the sidelines. People who suffer from them aren't interested in influencing others for their good. They're only interested in protecting the good they each have, in being for themselves rather than for anyone else.

Pride can also be seen in self-sufficiency. This kind of prideful man refuses to trust anyone because he believes that "if it's going to be, it's up to me." He feels he's got to constantly prove himself—that his identity is always on the line, and that if he has to depend on others, then his masculinity is compromised. He may do a lot of heroic things and he might act in a lot of heroic ways. But he is far too concerned with his own glory to be a hero.

Pride also shows itself in our self-righteousness. Most of

us think of self-righteousness horizontally. When others think they are better than we are and make a point of letting us know it, we describe them as "self-righteous." But self-righteousness also has a vertical dimension. When people are self-righteous in this sense, they think that all their good deeds will justify them and make them right before God.

The man trying to be self-righteous in the vertical sense is going to be exhausted. He has started spinning on the hamster wheel and he won't be able to stop. Every new situation he faces, every danger that he confronts, he's going to have to get it right because being right is all he has. He's not really trying to be someone else's hero. He's trying to be his own hero—trying to never let himself down because his life is dependent upon always being right.

Guys are trying hard to be saviors. But regardless of how much we get right, we're going to let *someone* down. We can't possibly go through life without disappointing others or without screwing up at least once. If we could, the world would be a lot better than it is.

In order to be a hero, we need a hero. We can't even be our own heroes, and we certainly don't have the energy or the power to make all the sacrifices our spouses', children's, and friends' souls thirst for. We need someone to be a sacrifice for us.

FOLLOWING THE TRUE HERO

Every little boy wants to be a hero. But boys also want to *have* heroes. They want someone they can look up to, imitate, and take cues from.

That was clear to me when my family and I got home from seeing the movie *The Avengers*. My son began putting together his bow and arrow so he could imitate Hawkeye, the arrow-shooting superhero from the film. My son knows he's not Hawkeye and that he falls short of the ideal. But that doesn't stop him from trying, even if he'll never get there.

At some point, though, men are disappointed by the older men in their lives. We tell ourselves that if this world is to have any heroes, it has got to be us. We start playing the messiah ourselves, trying to pull ourselves and everyone else around us up by the bootstraps.

That process isn't just exhausting—it's impossible. All the prescriptions, the to-do lists, the accountability groups, the therapists, the life coaches, the self-help books, and the business strategy books can't help us find the sort of satisfaction and completeness we desire. There aren't enough hours in the day and not enough counselors in the world to help us on the level that we need.

And even if there were, there is still the unquestionable fact that we are going to die someday. All our efforts might win us the immortality of fame, and we might build a financial empire that is passed down to our families, but even so, we won't be around to enjoy it.

Ask the guys who you think are heroes how they got there. Odds are, they'll laugh at the title because they know their own imperfections. People who do heroic things don't tout their awesomeness; instead, you'll hear them say things like, "I was just doing my duty," or "I was just doing what anyone would have done." We even expect that sort of self-effacing humility from our heroes. There's something unseemly about a man who builds a hospital for children, for instance, reminding everyone of the fact every chance he gets. But most genuine heroes know the faults in their own souls despite their good deeds.

We need a hero who can claim heroism not because he did his duty, but because he did more than his duty. We need someone who is perfect, who can sacrifice himself for us without us wondering if he did it because he's really only trying to exorcise his demons or simply get something from us. We need a hero whose humility is not simply rooted in recognizing his flaws and limitations but also in his submission to God. We need a hero who is interested in our good above all else, including his own life. When we see this sort of hero, then we can be free from the crushing obligation we feel to save ourselves and those around us, and we can be free to live out a new sort of life.

> WE NEED THE HEROISM OF A MAN WHO MANAGED TO BE PERFECT—AND WHO HAS THE POWER AND AUTHORITY OF GOD—SO THAT WE CAN BE SET FREE FROM THE DEMAND OF JUSTIFYING OURSELVES BEFORE HIM.

The good news is that we can have this sort of hero, and all we need to do is acknowledge our failures and our sins and entrust ourselves to him. We need the heroism of a man who managed to be perfect—and who has the power and authority of God—so that we can be set free from the demand of justifying ourselves before him. We need the true hero. We need Jesus.

Jesus is the true and perfect hero, the one who turned away from the comfort of his life in heaven and willingly entered history to die for our sins. As God, he had every right to continue to look in upon humanity from afar and leave us to ourselves.

But rather than standing apart, the Bible says that Jesus entered in and embraced a humility that was manifested in his willing embrace of death for our sake. He was not too proud to be shamed, mocked, scorned, and crucified in order to deliver humanity from our sins. He set aside his own interests for us.

JESUS IS THE TRUE AND PERFECT HERO, THE ONE WHO TURNED AWAY FROM THE COMFORT OF HIS LIFE IN HEAVEN AND WILLINGLY ENTERED HISTORY TO DIE FOR OUR SINS.

If ever there was a model for manhood, it's Jesus. The willingness to relentlessly and uncompromisingly pursue the good of those around him is unparalleled in human history. Jesus is the true man.

THE TRUE MAN: JESUS

A Determined Man

It's wrong to say that Jesus didn't face any obstacles or that he didn't understand the challenges and setbacks we face today. He had opponents at every turn who actively opposed his mission and his message. His first public sermon was preceded by a confrontation with Satan, who came to him and offered him immediate control over the entire earth. Yet despite every obstacle, Jesus remained focused on our good and on being a perfect sacrifice on our behalf.[2]

A Coachable Man

Jesus was the perfect teacher, but the Gospel of Luke describes him being led by the Holy Spirit.[3] He said that he did on earth whatever his Father did.[4] Jesus modeled humility for us by making it clear he was under the guidance and authority of God, the Father. When he was at his worst, wanting to avoid the suffering of the cross, Jesus said, "Not My will, but Yours, be done."[5]

A Disciplined Man

Jesus' life operated on a schedule, and he understood that certain things had to be reserved until the appropriate time. His worship, for instance, followed the Jewish calendar. He knew that his final destination was the cross, and he was disciplined in what he said, reserving the right thing for the right time. He knew that once the sun came up, he would be mobbed by the crowds, so he made it his practice to get up early to be with his Father and get instruction for the day.[6] He knew where he was headed, and he was disciplined in his approach to getting there.

A Working Man

In one of the most amusing scenes from *The Passion of the Christ* (actually, maybe the *only* amusing scene), Jesus makes a table and chairs and Mary, his mother, has no idea what they are. Tables and chairs didn't exist in Jesus' day, but Jesus is able to make them because he's God. While the moment isn't in the Bible, it does remind us that Jesus was a workingman. He was trained as a carpenter, he hung out with fishermen, and he had friends who were wealthy businessmen. More than that, he knew what his job was—to die for the sins of the world and to proclaim the message of repentance of sin and faith in God. And he was single-minded in his pursuit of it.

A Content Man

Jesus had all that anyone could possibly imagine before he became incarnate as a man. But he relinquished everything for our sake and entered into a world of hardship, of limitation, and of suffering and death. That's an astonishing fact, and it suggests that at heart Jesus' contentment was secure not because of his circumstances and surroundings but because of his ongoing relationship with the Father. He didn't need anything more than that.

A Family Man

In his final act on the cross, Jesus entrusted the care of his mother to his good friend John. He was aware of his responsibilities as a son and knew that even though he was God, he needed to fulfill them.[7] But more than that, Jesus' identity as the Son of God the Father was the basis for his entire life. He began a new family—those who are called Christians—and still calls those who believe in him brothers and sisters. He is and was a family man from beginning to end.

A Devoted Man

One of the strangest metaphors in the Bible is that Jesus is the groom and that his people, the church, are his bride. Throughout the entire Bible, God related to his people as a good husband. He is faithful, forgiving, and sacrificial. He cherishes us enough to give everything for our good. He knows us intimately, knowing even our sitting and our rising and every thought that is on our hearts. He is deeply devoted to his people and cares for us.

A Connected Man

Jesus had followers who are known as the disciples. They learned from him as a padawan might learn from a Jedi. Their job was to soak up as much as they could, to imitate him, and obey his commands. But in a remarkable statement, Jesus opened the door for his disciples to become more than followers. He invited them to be *friends*, to be equals with him in his work, in his rest, in all the benefits and joys that are his—even as the Son of God.[8]

An Emotional Man

When Jesus found out his friend Lazarus had died, the Bible records his response in two powerful words: "Jesus wept" (John 11:35). When the religious leaders of his day were selling things in the temple, Jesus overturned their tables and angrily whipped them with cords (Matt. 21:12)! Though he wasn't ruled by his emotions, Jesus refused to deny them either. Jesus felt things deeply, but he also felt them rightly.

A Fighting Man

Jesus won the war to end all wars (literally). He stared death in the face and overcame it. He vanquished it and continues to vanquish anything else that would dare oppose him. He is ever victorious, always triumphant, and glorious in his strength. And he fights on our behalf, coming to our aid and defense and triumphing over the one who would destroy our souls. His character is perfect—but the Bible suggests that even he had to overcome temptations and trials, which would have tested his character and caused him to fight for his own goodness.[9]

A PERFECT SAVIOR

Jesus is much more than an example to us in all these things. He is the one who enables us to become like him because he frees us from the guilt we feel when we see how short we have fallen of his perfection. We were created to be true men—men of courage and industry and goodness. But that glory has been buried because of our ongoing rebellion against the Creator. It's not just that we can't be perfect; it's that we don't want to be perfect and so we hate the One who is.

We need forgiveness for these sins and to be made new so we can fulfill all that we have been created to be. That is what Jesus offers us. And if we will open ourselves to his mercy at the Cross, then we can begin to live in the integrity of acknowledging our imperfections without letting them drive us to despair. We can embrace the hope that we will someday no longer struggle as we now do because Jesus rose from the dead and has worked renewal in our hearts. And we can begin the long, slow, and pleasantly painful process of letting Jesus dig through our bitterness, our anger, our desire to control others, our pride, and our envy to uncover the true and glorious manhood that lies somewhere deep within the hearts of us all.

Jesus is not only the true man. He is also the only true Savior.

You may have a sense that you need this hero in your life. You are tired of trying to save yourself with your own good works and your own good intentions. You realize that you will never be good enough to get to God. If that is you, consider the following two commands and prayer.

Repent: The Bible tells us that we have violated God's laws and that we need forgiveness from the good and great lawgiver.[10]

To repent means that you ask for God's mercy and forgiveness for your past sins.

Believe: The Bible says that to believe in Jesus is to bank on his work to save you instead of banking on your work to save you. To believe is to trust Jesus' work to save you. To believe means you cease trying to be your own hero and savior and rest in Jesus as your hero and savior.[11]

Prayer: If this all makes sense to you, pray with these words: "God, I see that I am so sinful that I can never save myself. I accept the gift of your Son, who lived perfectly so I don't have to be perfect; who died brutally so I don't have to be punished; and who rose from death so I don't have to live in my own strength."

If you prayed this prayer authentically, your sins are totally blotted out and the righteousness of God is applied to you because of Christ! Also, the Holy Spirit—the third person of the Trinity—is now living in you to empower you to become more and more free of sin and more like Jesus in your character.

Now, read this last chapter as a newly forgiven man.

TWELVE

LIVING AS THE FORGIVEN MAN

"OKAY, NOW WHAT?" YOU MIGHT BE SAYING. "ALL THIS sounds great. But what should I do next? What sort of changes should I make beyond those I've already tried?"

The fact is that if you try to do everything this book suggests, you're only going to get frustrated and tired. Take care of your family. Be emotional, but don't let emotions govern you. Love your job, but not too much. Train yourself rather than merely try. I've attempted to get beneath the surface of these ideas and more in order to examine issues of the heart, but it's still easy to simply hear the prescriptions and then tell ourselves that change will happen with new information and the right techniques. If things were that simple, you would be keeping all your New Year's resolutions, which, let's face it, you probably aren't.

Change is hard. Once ruts of sinful behavior are formed, they are difficult to escape. We return again and again to what seems familiar to us because it's known and comfortable, even if it's destructive. And most of the time we are oblivious. Like gravity, sin can't be seen or touched—but it exerts force on us, pulling us back to earth and returning us to the life we are trying to escape.

"Nothing is impossible with God" is one of my favorite Bible verses (Luke 1:37 NLT). Conversely, change is impossible without God. And God has come near to us, becoming a man like us. Jesus didn't come as a professional athlete or a head of state. He didn't come as a doctor or therapist, as a guru or guide. He came as a carpenter and a preacher, as a man who was perfect and who died for us.

Jesus is the true man, but he's also the true God. And when we trust in him, we are given the gift of salvation. We are also given real power to change our lives because we have been given a divine power source—the Holy Spirit.[1] In giving us himself, God gives us new life. And that gives us hope that we can be different as men. We don't have to be trapped in the same patterns of rejecting our responsibility, of laziness and sloth, of anger, fear, and frustration. The life Jesus gives us is true life, eternal life, but also just life. It's freedom, joy, peace, love, courage, and whatever we need to be like him.

Change is possible. But even with Jesus, it's not easy and it won't be instantaneous. It will take a lifetime of trusting, walking with God, confessing, and repenting of sin to become the sort of men God has called us to be. True manhood doesn't mean being perfect ourselves; it means trusting in Christ's perfection for us. True manhood doesn't mean getting everything right; it means having the courage to say when we get things wrong and the confidence that comes from receiving our acceptance from God in Christ.[2]

That doesn't mean we should just sit on our hands and do nothing, though. We can confess and repent and mourn for our sins while deepening our awareness of God's forgiveness for us. The life of Jesus exposes our sins *as* sin. They aren't simply problems, hang-ups, or flaws that get in the way of our happiness as men or that make others around us uneasy or afraid—though they are those too. They are also offenses against God himself, ways in which we reject him as our Father, Lord, and Creator. When we meet Jesus, we realize that we don't have problems—we *are* the problem. It's we who are broken, and broken people can't fix themselves.

> TRUE MANHOOD DOESN'T MEAN BEING PERFECT OURSELVES; IT MEANS TRUSTING IN CHRIST'S PERFECTION FOR US.

In Christ, though, we are forgiven men. We are men whose sins have been covered by the perfect sacrifice of Jesus. This means we don't need to walk in fear or anxiety or strive for our own glory any longer. We are forgiven, set free from the pain of our past, and empowered to face the future with all its challenges and promises.

Here's some of what it means to live life as a forgiven man.

FORGIVEN MEN FORGIVE OTHERS

When Jesus' disciples asked him how they should pray, he answered with a prayer that has set the template for Christians' prayer from the moment it was written down.

Our Father in heaven,
Hallowed be Your name.
Your kingdom come,
Your will be done
On earth as it is in heaven.
Give us this day our daily bread.
And forgive us our debts,
As we forgive our debtors.
And do not lead us into temptation,
But deliver us from the evil one. (Matt. 6:9–15)

Notice that Jesus included asking for forgiveness *and* our forgiveness of others. The two are tied together. Those who are forgiven have the power to forgive. And those who practice the power of forgiveness of others will experience the same power from God in their own lives.

Many of us men have much to forgive our fathers for. We may at points in our lives be angry with them or frustrated by them. You may have realized through reading this book how badly they equipped you to face the world and may be allowing the seeds of bitterness to take root in your heart. You might justify it by saying that it is deserved, that if your father had done a better job, you wouldn't have any reason to be bitter.

But that sort of anger toward others only erodes our strength as men. It doesn't make us more manly to not forgive our fathers. There is no need to embrace the lyrics of "Cat's in the Cradle" as our disposition toward our dads.[3] Bitterness shifts responsibility for our lives to them rather than ourselves. Bitterness keeps us victims. When we forgive our fathers, however, we release them from having to carry the responsibility of providing for our happiness. And that means we are responsible for our own lives, for our own future and legacy.

That is why it's important to take the step of forgiveness when we experience God's forgiveness. The power we have in Christ allows us to take responsibility for ourselves. It sets us free from sin, but not free from our responsibility for it. Christ's death on the cross takes our punishment and our guilt—but we can only recognize him as a substitute if we recognize that we deserve to be there instead. Once we recognize that we are responsible for our sins but released from them, we can properly release others in the same way.

The more we gossip about those who have hurt us, the more we resent them, the more we scorn them or slander them, the more the grudge will take root in our hearts, eventually blossoming into soul-crushing bitterness. If we really enter into forgiving others, we will suffer. We will hurt. It does not feel good to let go of our sense that we should have vindication, that our complaints should be heard, and that we should have our own way. But as forgiveness works its way into our hearts and out toward others, we will be free from our anger and hurt and free to love others again.

> BITTERNESS SHIFTS RESPONSIBILITY FOR OUR LIVES TO THEM RATHER THAN OURSELVES. BITTERNESS KEEPS US VICTIMS.

FORGIVEN MEN FREE OTHERS

When we men are setting the standard of perfection and holding everyone else around us to it, we can become manipulative and controlling. But when we walk in the forgiveness we have in Christ, we set others free to be themselves. In being freed from our pasts, we free others from being held captive to their pasts. Because we no longer have to be perfect, we no longer have to require perfection of others.

As we have discussed, our sin has a relational dimension. Manhood isn't something we pursue because we want fulfilling lives for ourselves, to make our own experience of the world more awesome and glorious. True manhood affects others. When men act like men, everyone else around is free to be who they are.

Rather than treat our friends as status symbols or stepping-stones for our own advancement and prestige, we will free them to pursue their goals. Our friends relax and are free to share with us their deepest hopes and fears. Rather than constantly justifying our shortcomings with our wives, we can listen and respond. Our wives will be free to correct us without concern of retaliation. Rather than treating our children as tokens to show the world what good parents we are, we will treat them as little people who have their own plans, desires, and dreams for the world. Our children are free to fail without the dread of a disapproving dad.

Forgiven men free others to be themselves because we have been set free.

FORGIVEN MEN KEEP REPENTING

Through the course of this book, I have highlighted various sins men commit and have tried to explain why they are so destructive to us and to those around us. But for the sake of clarity, let's revisit a few of them.

Envy

Envy isn't just wanting someone's stuff; it is wanting someone's life. It means being angry about their happiness and wishing that we had it and they didn't. Those who are envious are sad when others rejoice and glad when others are upset.

When we begin to walk with Jesus, though, we are set free from envy and introduced into a life of empathy. We are empowered to truly celebrate with those who celebrate rather than secretly rooting for their demise.

The thing about envy is that it hides. It hides in our daydreams about being a rock star, professional athlete, or the boss. It hides in the thoughts that are played in HD in our heads when a colleague gets a promotion or a friend gets a bigger house. Our problem with envy is not with Bono or Tom Brady; it is with those who are just a *bit* better off than we are.

Pride

Pride is related to envy. I am not talking about pride in its popular definition: "feeling satisfaction about what you have accomplished." I am talking about pride theologically. This kind of pride is the belief that we are the most important thing in the universe and that the stars and the sun all revolve around us.

When we think of pride we tend to think about arrogance— the guy who talks about himself all the time. But we don't often recognize it in the guy who spends his days worrying about his own success even if he never says a word about it. They are both consumed with themselves, but their pride takes different forms. Pride is ultimately an inordinate focus on the self.

One of the most pervasive forms pride takes is self-pity, particularly among men whose upbringings are less than ideal. It's easy for guys who face their pasts to end up wallowing because things didn't go as well as they had wanted, or they feel that they're now "behind" where other guys are. But that sort of self-pity is simply the reverse of thinking that we're entitled to a particular sort of upbringing—a sense of entitlement that might be a sort of pride.

John Piper describes the relationship between self-pity and pride this way:

> Boasting is the response of pride to success. Self-pity is the response of pride to suffering. Boasting says, "I deserve admiration because I have achieved so much." Self-pity says, "I deserve admiration because I have sacrificed so much." Boasting is the voice of pride in the heart of the strong. Self-pity is the voice of pride in the heart of the weak . . . The need that self-pity feels does not come from a sense of unworthiness but from a sense of unrecognized worthiness. It is the response of unapplauded pride.[4]

When we trust in Jesus, our lives become all about him, not about our own advancement, success, performance, or anything else that we think our existence depends upon. *His* perfection and power are the keys to our lives, not our own. And the perfect man whose life we are given didn't seize the keys of power when they were offered to him, but died on a cross on behalf of others. He didn't wallow in self-pity when asked to die for the salvation of the world. He struggled in facing up to it, but when it came down to it, he told the Father "Not my will, but Yours, be done." Because even for Jesus, it's not about him but about the glory that is given to God the Father. As writer Tim Elmore said, "Humility isn't thinking less of yourself, it is thinking of yourself less."[5]

Lust

Earlier I said that our problems aren't simply corrosive to other people but are sins against God. That's true here, too, even though it often might not seem like it. Where it's clear how other sins, like pride, are ways of actually offending against God himself, what does lust have to do with God?

The problem with lust goes deeper than an attachment to porn. If anything, porn is the manifestation of what is already in the heart and has taken over the mind. Most guys don't start their lustful thoughts by looking at porn; they turn on the porn because they've imagined themselves and women in a particular way, so that porn becomes the nearest substitute for their thrills. It's a cheap and deadly trick, but all sin is. Many guys who don't even look at porn still struggle with lust, even though they might not say so. The guy who looks at a woman while walking through the mall and momentarily imagines her in a sexual situation is lusting—even though she'll never know it and would almost certainly be creeped out by it. Lust isn't only wrong when it "hurts someone." It's wrong all the time.

Lust is a monster, and the more you feed it, the larger it gets. In the Bible, David was God's anointed king over Israel. Yet the Bible recounts a moment of his shame, as he committed an affair with the wife of one of his generals. The adultery happened partly because David had fed his lust beforehand. David had been commanded not to multiply his wives (Deut. 17:16–18), but he disobeyed that command and sated his sexual desire with several wives and concubines. He did not bring his sexual desires under control—he gave them free expression. And when he was placed in a situation to have an affair with another man's wife, he had no internal power to resist.

Still, lust is a sin against God because God cares deeply about women and wants them to be revered, cherished, and respected—not treated as objects of gratification. When men reduce women to sex objects even in our minds, we not only dehumanize women but we offend the God who made them in his image. He loves women and cherishes them much more than we realize.

This is why here, too, Christian men need to be in a posture of ongoing confession and repentance for the sins we commit. The forgiveness we have in Christ covers these sins—but as they come up to us, that forgiveness allows us to acknowledge them and live in the light of God's grace. We don't need to hide our sins or our struggles; we can be honest and forthright about them, recognizing that the mercy we have in Jesus is everlasting and our lives will never be the same.

Anger

Anger is a feeling of displeasure that shows itself in a desire to fight back at a perceived injustice. Guys get angry when they see something wrong. Anger is a hard sin to pin down because we rename it. We make it sound more benign by saying we got "frustrated" or "passionate." We excuse ourselves by saying that we are too direct, or that we tell it like it is. Those may be true enough. But if beneath our behavior is actually an angry heart, then we are probably hiding areas of our lives from the long reach of God's transformative love.

Not every sort of anger is wrong, of course, as I mentioned in the chapter on the emotional man. Sometimes it's good to get angry. If injustices are real and not only perceived, then we should allow ourselves to feel angry about them—provided that we do not allow our anger to take the form of bitterness or allow it to overwhelm us.

But when we feel anger, we have to ask ourselves an important question: What are we defending? Many times, what we're defending isn't an injustice at all but only our own sense of glory, vanity, pride, and entitlement. We get angry when others don't treat us the way we think we should be treated, or when others don't do what we think they should do. We get angry when things aren't easy for us, when there is more difficulty in our path than we expected at the beginning.

The reality is that if we don't root out these things, then the anger we let in will rot into bitterness, explode through wrath, or seep out as we seethe with malice toward those around us. But in order to let go of such sinful anger, we have to let go of our sense of control and domination of the world. It is the acknowledgment that we are not the most important things in the universe that frees us from being angry when people don't treat us the way we want. When men relinquish their entitlement to a particular way of life, then they can let go of their anger at not having it.

We need Jesus, though, to displace us at the center and to make our lives about his life and not our own. We need his forgiveness to come and work with our anger, to help us pause in the moment. We need Jesus to move a new heart into the place where our current one is, to fill us with a righteous anger toward the injustices of rape, poverty, racism, and abuse, rather than simply being consumed by the smallness of our own lives. We need to see that God the Father took out all his anger (wrath) on his Son for our sins, which will help us deal with our anger.

FORGIVEN MEN GO TO CHURCH

I get it. I mean, I really get it. You don't like church and you don't understand what goes on there. I mean, they *sing* there, right? And the last time you were caught singing publicly was karaoke after seven too many beers. Some of you have been to churches that were effeminate, as if you walked into the wrong store in the mall. It was uncomfortable and disorienting and I get why you didn't want to go back.

The truth is that you aren't going to be able to do this alone. Church isn't about what we get out of church but what we bring into it—ourselves, our worship, our service for God to others. Finding a community that lives out the fullness of the life that God has for the church is hard, but possible. I've described what I think is a biblical vision for the church with my friend Matt Carter in *For the City.* But a community of people who believe the good news that Jesus set us free from sin and who are serving their friends and neighbors is absolutely indispensable.

I've made it pretty clear that true men don't live in isolation from others. They live with others. They are mentored by other men and mentor other men. Every guy needs someone encouraging him to push forward and be all that God has called him to be, and also someone he is pouring himself into. Guys need communities of friends who are willing to challenge them and fight with them for their character and practical holiness. And the church is supposed to be the backbone of that community—the place where the good news of Jesus is proclaimed in such a way that it permeates men's friendships.

Many of you guys are coming from homes that didn't equip you well to face the challenges of this life. You had absent fathers who neglected you because they were scared and hadn't been equipped themselves. You're looking for something deeper and more permanent. The good news is that the church is supposed to function like a family (Acts 2:42–47). Emotional, physical, and spiritual support are all part of the church's gift to those who enter into it. And if your local church isn't providing that support, then it might be time to diagnose the degree to which its members are genuinely serving one another in love.

Forgiven Men Serve

Church gets a ton more interesting when you serve. Most guys who go to church never get beyond attending the service on Sunday morning. This is why they are spiritually bored. The church has a life beyond its worship services, and guys need to get involved in that life. Jesus calls the church to be on mission for him, to preach the gospel to neighbors and nations, to serve the poor and the orphan and the widow.

In a letter the apostle Paul wrote to the early Christians at Philippi, he exhorts them to "count others as more significant than [themselves]" (Phil. 2:3 ESV). He points to Jesus as an example. Though he was equal with God, Jesus humbled himself and became human with all our frailties and infirmities.

He served us with such a love that we killed him for it. And Paul wants us as Christians to serve just as Christ did. He wants us to treat other people's interests and needs as more important than our own. He wants us to live for Jesus and live for others—to love God and love others rather than being consumed with ourselves.

Men who are forgiven also have the power to serve others. And if they will place themselves in situations where they have to serve, men will find themselves with the desire to serve others as well. Everyone is busy. The question is whether our busy lives will prevent us from living out the love that God has placed in our hearts. Whether in the home, in the church, or in our friendships, we are called to lay down our lives for others and pursue their welfare ahead of our own.

Men, you are gifted. You have something to contribute. God wants to use you to do more than just make money, advance your careers, and love your families. He wants to work through you to make a difference in your neighborhoods, communities, and world. God will work in you as he works through you. Stop waiting to be perfect before you step out and serve others. God is with you, and he is a good dad and won't give up on you if you fail to eat your vegetables. Trust him entirely, and sacrificially serve those around you.

ACKNOWLEDGMENTS

I WANT TO THANK THE FIRST AND MOST IMPORTANT dude in my life, my dad. My dad is in the ninth inning of his life and has done "the best he could with the tools that he was given." He has taught me so much and I would not be where I am without him.

My wife has tested every theory of manhood that I have ever thought of in the furnace of a twenty-year marriage. I am blown away by how well she knows me and even more by how much she still loves me. Amie, you are indeed a "mystery to be explored" and I look forward to the next season of our lives together.

Having three daughters humbles a man greatly. All three of you girls are unique and wonderful. I enjoy you all just as you are. My hope and prayer is that you will find a man who is truly masculine and is able to love you the way your hearts desire.

I want to thank the board of elders of The Journey. These are the men whom I have submitted my life and work to. We have had really hard times and really sweet times. Without them,

I would not have had the time or the spiritual and emotional strength to lead, speak, or write. These men are the embodiment of tough and tender in my life.

My friend Matthew Anderson worked tirelessly on this project. All the while he was finishing a book of his own and preparing to move across the pond to get his PhD at Oxford. Our sessions together—mostly of us talking, philosophizing, and defining what a man actually should be—were the foundation for the content of this book. His research and constant attention to detail made this book so much better than if I had set out alone. I have to say I was really sad when our time on this work was completed. Put simply, Matthew made this book better because he cares about men being better and because Matthew is a better man than most.

I want to thank the lead pastors of The Journey, men whom I desire to be like. You read the manuscript and made great suggestions. More than that, you have given me a "band of brothers" to celebrate and serve with as we seek to fight the good fight for the souls of men.

I also want to acknowledge my assistant, Jeremy Burrows. Jeremy has been in my life since he was twelve years old. I have seen him grow up before my eyes. I am so impressed by the way he loves his wife and his son. Jeremy serves me by handling myriad details so that, in his words, "Darrin can focus on the things that Darrin should be focused on." Jeremy is the hardest worker I have ever met and always serves me and others with a smile. This book and the work that God has called me to is made possible by his joyful service.

NOTES

Introduction

1. Sons with fathers who have committed crimes are two times more likely to have a criminal conviction themselves, and a second criminal conviction by their father increases their odds by 32 percent. (These numbers are even higher for daughters.) Similarly, a child is six times as likely to get a college degree if his or her father has one. See Randi Hjalmarsson and Matthew Lindquist, "Like Godfather, Like Son: Exploring the Intergenerational Nature of Crime," *The Journal of Human Resources* 47, no. 2 (2012): 550–582; Heather Sipsma, Katie Brooks Biello, Heather Cole-Lewis, and Trace Kershaw, "Like Father, Like Son: The Intergenerational Cycle of Adolescent Fatherhood," *American Journal of Public Health* 100, no. 3 (2010): 517–524.
2. J. R. R. Tolkien (novel), Fran Walsh, Philipa Boyens, and Peter Jackson (screenplay), *The Lord of the Rings: The Fellowship of the Ring*, directed by Peter Jackson (New Line Cinema, 2001).
3. Tom Schulman, *Dead Poets Society*, directed by Peter Weir (Touchstone Pictures, 1989).

Chapter 1: Get It Done: Become a Determined Man

1. This is a paraphrase.
2. This is a common problem. Generational patterns tend to

emerge over time. See, for instance, Heather Sipsma, Katie
Brooks Biello, Heather Cole-Lewis, and Trace Kershaw, "Like
Father, Like Son: The Intergenerational Cycle of Adolescent
Fatherhood," *American Journal of Public Health* 100, no. 3
(2010): 517–524.

3. Jennifer Brown, "Quitters Never Win: The (Adverse) Incentive
Effects of Competing with Superstars," *Journal of Political
Economy*, 2011, 119 (5): 982–1013.

4. Farrell Evans, "Tiger Woods Still Looking For Solution," ESPN
.com, May 3, 2012, http://espn.go.com/golf/story/_/id/7881769
/tiger-woods-looking-solution.

5. Amazingly, this talk seems to be still available on his old
church's website. See "Ephesians 5:22–24: Spirit-Filled Families,
Part 1," available at http://www.preceptaustin.org/new_page
_28.htm. Accessed March 29, 2013.

Chapter 2: Pay Attention and Learn Something: Become a Coachable Man

1. Matt Damon and Ben Affleck, *Good Will Hunting*, directed by
Gus Van Sant (Miramax, 1997).

2. Judd Apatow, *Knocked Up*, directed by Judd Apatow (Universal
Pictures, 1997).

3. "*kenodoxía*." This word has the two senses: a. "delusion" and
b. "conceit." Only b. occurs in the New Testament (Phil. 2:3),
though we find both in the apostolic fathers (a. in Hermas,
Similitudes 8.9.3, and b. in Hermas, *Mandates* 8.5). Friedrich
G. Kittel and G. W. Bromiley, *Theological Dictionary of the New
Testament* (Grand Rapids, MI: W. B. Eerdmans, 1995), 426–427.

Chapter 3: Train, Don't Just Try: Become a Disciplined Man

1. Rick Rescorla's story can be found in the History Channel's
documentary, "The Man who Predicted 9/11," available at http://
www.youtube.com/watch?v=1UcJo7dxOOU. Accessed March 29,
2013.

2. The above paragraphs and citations are based on the History Channel documentary about his life, "The Man who Predicted 9/11." Available online at http://www.youtube.com /watch?v=1UcJo7dxOOU. Accessed August 9, 2012.

3. H. L. Mencken, *A Second Mencken Chrestomathy*, ed. Terry Teachout (New York: Knopf, 2006), 67.

4. Pamela Paul, *Pornified* (New York: Owl Books, 2005).

5. While he doesn't describe the effects of porn this way, psychologist William Todd Schultz has suggested that the pornification of the mind extends beyond just how we think beyond sex. William Todd Schultz, "The Pornification of Human Consciousness," PsychologyToday.com, March 26, 2009, http://www.psychologytoday .com/blog/genius-and-madness/200903/the-pornification-human -consciousness. Accessed August 9, 2012.

6. Such intense experiences also release a flood of drugs in the brain that prove themselves to be addictive. As journalist Stephen Kotler wrote, "The particular neurochemicals produced by action sports are far more potent than any single drug around and— since one cannot cocktail massive amounts of speed, cocaine, and heroin without ending up dead—adrenaline sports are really the only way to get this kind of taste." See "The Addictive Nature of Adrenaline Sports," PsychologyToday.com, http://www .psychologytoday.com/blog/the-playing-field/200803/the -addicitve-nature-adrenaline-sport. Accessed August 9, 2012.

7. John Ortberg, *The Life You've Always Wanted: Expanded Edition* (Grand Rapids: Zondervan, 2002), 47.

8. Theodore Roosevelt, "The Strenuous Life" (speech before the Hamilton Club, Chicago, IL, April 10, 1899), in Thomas Herbert Russell, *Life and Work of Theodore Roosevelt* (New York: L. H. Walter, 1919), 173.

Chapter 4: Love Your Work:
Become a Working Man

1. Theologian Wayne Grudem defines *sin* as "any failure to conform to the moral law of God in act, attitude, or nature." Wayne Grudem, *Systematic Theology* (Grand Rapids: Zondervan, 2009), 1254.

2. Leland Ryken et al., eds, *The Dictionary of Biblical Imagery* (Madison: InterVarsity Press, 1998), 9–10. See also the entry in the *Oxford English Dictionary*: "vice-regent, n" OED Online, March 2013, Oxford University Press. http://ezproxy.ouls.ox .ac.uk:2277/view/Entry/223153?redirectedFrom=viceregent. Accessed March 29, 2013.

3. Andy Crouch, *Culture Making: Recovering our Creative Calling* (Downers Grove, IL: IVP Books, 2008), 75.

4. When men are not employed, both husband and wife are more likely to leave the marriage. This may have to do with historical expectations about male-female roles, but given the backdrop of how men are made, it may also indicate less emotional satisfaction among men with their lives when not employed. See Liana Sayer et al., "She Left, He Left: How Employment and Satisfaction Affect Men's and Women's Decisions to Leave Marriages," *American Journal of Sociology* 116, no. 6 (May 2011), 1982–2018. What's more, while the research is now somewhat dated, there is some evidence that how much women work has no effect on their health, but that the husband's work hours show a positive effect on men's health. See R. M. Stolzenberg, "It's About Time and Gender: Spousal Employment and Health," *American Journal of Sociology* 107, no. 1 (July 2001), 61–100.

5. Chuck Palahniuk and Jim Uhls, *Fight Club*, directed by David Fincher (Fox 2000 Pictures, 1999).

6. Census figures from 1900 available at http://www.census.gov /population/www/documentation/twps0027/tab13.txt. Accessed March 29, 2013.

7. Carolyn Heger, "Answers CEO Karandish Named Entrepreneur of the Year," *St. Louis Business Journal,* June 6, 2012, http://www .bizjournals.com/stlouis/news/2012/06/06/answerscom -ceo-karandish-named.html.

8. William McGuinness, "Half of Recent College Grads Work Jobs That Don't Require a Degree," *Huffington Post,* January 29, 2013, http://www.huffingtonpost.com/2013/01/29/underemployed -overeducated_n_2568203.html/. The unemployment rate for

people who did not attend college is double that of recent college graduates too.

9. Daniel Buckszpan, "Economy: The Man-cession and the He-covery," January 27, 2012, http://usatoday30.usatoday.com /money/economy/story/2012-01-29/cnbc-mancession /52826370/1.

10. A study by Shell found that people entering retirement at fifty-five were more likely to die earlier than those who retired at sixty-five (even accounting for ill health). However, there are other studies that suggest there is no difference in mortality rates. See Shan P. Thai, Judy K Wendt, Robin P. Donnelly, Geert de Jong, and Farah S. Ahmed, "Age at Retirement and Long Term Survival of an Industrial Population: Prospective Cohort Study," *BMJ: British Medical Journal* 2005, 331 (7523): 995.

11. Walter Kirn and Jason Reitman, *Up in the Air,* directed by Jason Reitman (Paramount, 2009).

12. Joe Strauss, "Holliday Wants to be Leader by Example," *St. Louis Post-Dispatch,* March 5, 2012, http://www.stltoday.com /sports/baseball/professional/holliday-wants-to-be-leader -by-example/article_bda52b74-95df-5869-ac13-985ecf6dc929 .html.

Chapter 5: Get Satisfaction: Become a Content Man

1. Josh Grossberg, "David Arquette Celebrates His Bar Mitzvah in Israel," Eonline.com, June 11, 2012, http://www.eonline.com /news/322525/david-arquette-celebrates-his-bar-mitzvah-in -israel-finally-i-m-a-man.

2. Charles William Eliot, ed., *Blaise Pascal: Thoughts, Letters, and Minor Works* (New York: P. F. Collier and Son, 1910), 138.

3. Owen Strachan, "R. C. Sproul Jr. on the Death of his Wife," Owen Strachan (blog), May 5, 2012, http://owenstrachan .com/2012/05/05/r-c-sproul-jr-on-the-death-of-his-wife/.

4. David Brooks, "The Organization Kid," *The Atlantic,* April,

2001, http://www.theatlantic.com/magazine/archive/2001/04
/the-organization-kid/302164/.

5. For an overview of the literature, see Patrick F. Fagan, "A Poison in the Home," *Catholic World Report,* May 9, 2011. Available at http://www.catholicworldreport.com/Item/605/a _poison_in_the_home.aspx#.UVWOIasd6jI. Accessed March 29, 2013.

6. C. S. Lewis, *The Problem of Pain* (New York: HarperCollins, 2001), 93.

Chapter 6: Love a Woman:
Become a Devoted Man

1. Court Crandall et al., *Old School,* directed by Todd Phillips (DreamsWorks, 2003).

2. Anna North, "Princeton Alums, State Dept. Staffer Run Revolting Sex Contest," Jezebel.com, January 3, 2011, http:// jezebel.com/5723470/princeton-alums-state-dept-staffer -compete-in-revolting-sex-contest.

3. Margaret Hartmann, "Frat Email Explains Women Are 'Targets,' Not 'Actual People,'" Jezebel.com, March 8, 2011, http://jezebel.com/5779905/usc-frat-guys-email-explains -women-are-targets-not-actual-people-like-us-men.

4. "Karen Owen's PowerPoint List Rocks Duke Campus, Goes Viral," AolNews.com, October 7, 2010, http://www.aolnews .com/2010/10/07/karen-owens-powerpoint-list-troubling-on -many-levels/.

5. Simon Rogers, "The Top 100 Bestselling Books of All Time: How Does Fifty Shades of Grey Compare?" *The Guardian,* August 9, 2012, http://www.guardian.co.uk/news/datablog /2012/aug/09/best-selling-books-all-time-fifty-shades -grey-compare.

6. D. Zillman and J. Bryant, "Pornography's Impact on Sexual Satisfaction," *Journal of Applied Social Psychology* 18, (1998): 438–453.

7. Wenham, G. J. "Bath, Bathing," in D. R. W. Wood, I. H.

Marshall, A. R. Millard, J. I. Packer & D. J. Wiseman (Eds.), *New Bible Dictionary* (3rd ed.) (Leicester, England; Downers Grove, IL: InterVarsity Press, 1996), 125.

8. Men are improving their life expectancy faster than women, though. (Michael Murray, "Life Expectancy for Men Outpacing Women, Says New Study," ABC News, June 16, 2011, http://abcnews.go.com/Health/life-expectancy-men-outpacing-women-study/story?id=13850055.) On the pain tolerance, this hasn't been scientifically demonstrated. But the persistence of the myth is itself interesting.

9. Ephesians 5:25.

10. Chas Danner, "Believe Your Eyes," *The Dish*, August 7, 2012, http://andrewsullivan.thedailybeast.com/2012/08/believe-your-eyes.html?utm_medium=feed&utm_campaign=Feed:+andrewsullivan/rApM+(The+Daily+Dish)&utm_source=buffer&buffer_share=ef795.

11. Cheryl Wetzstein, "U.S. Marriage Rate Continues Decline; Men Tie Knot Later," *Washington Times,* February 5, 2012, http://www.washingtontimes.com/news/2012/feb/5/us-marriage-rate-continues-decline-men-tie-knot-la/?page=all.

12. The interview has been put on YouTube. It's available at http://www.youtube.com/watch?v=YqLWQ0oHhBE. Accessed March 29, 2013.

Chapter 7: Love Kids: Become a Family Man

1. Morgan Evans, "The 9 Most Awful (And Awesome) Anti-Drug PSAs Ever Made," *Huffington Post*, May 31, 2010, http://www.huffingtonpost.com/2010/03/31/the-9-most-awful-and-awes_n_514991.html#s76273&title=I_Learned_It.

2. "confess, v." OED Online, March 2013, Oxford University Press. 29 March 2013, http://ezproxy.ouls.ox.ac.uk:2277/view/Entry/38766?redirectedFrom=confess.

3. G. K. Chesterton, *What's Wrong with the World* (New York: Dodd, Mead and Company, 1912), 294.

Chapter 8: Say, "I Love You, Man": The Connected Man

1. The difficulty of making new friends was highlighted by the *New York Times* in Alex Williams, "Friends of a Certain Age," *New York Times,* July 13, 2012, http://www.nytimes.com/2012 /07/15/fashion/the-challenge-of-making-friends-as-an-adult .html?pagewanted=all. What's more, there is some evidence to suggest that men generally experience more loneliness than women. Or if the levels are equal, men are less willing to admit it. See Shelley Boyrs and Daniel Perman, "Gender Differences in Loneliness," *Personality and Social Psychology Bulletin* 11–1 (March 1985): 63–74. While the study is dated and additional studies have qualified the research, its core findings seem to hold. See Liesl M. Heinrich and Eleonora Gullone, "The Clinical Significance of Loneliness: A Literature Review," *Clinical Psychology Review* 26 (2006): 695–718.

2. Janet Kornblum, "Study: 25% of Americans Have No One to Confide In," *USA Today,* June 22, 2006, http://usatoday30 .usatoday.com/news/nation/2006-06-22-friendship_x.htm.

3. C. S. Lewis, *The Weight of Glory* (New York: HarperCollins, 2001), 141–158.

4. Ibid., 55.

5. C. S. Lewis, *The Four Loves* (New York: Harcourt Books, 1988), 61.

6. C. S. Lewis used this imagery in *The Four Loves.* There is some evidence that men tend to be "task focused" in their friendships while women are not. See Shawn Patrick and John Beckenbaugh, "Male Perceptions of Intimacy: A Qualitative Study," *The Journal of Men's Studies,* 17, no. 1 (Winter 2009): 47–56. See also Mayta A. Caldwell and Letitia Anne Peplau, "Sex Differences in Same-Sex Friendship," *Sex Roles.* 8 (7), 1982, pages 721–732.

Chapter 9: Feel Something Without Crying at Everything: The Emotional Man

1. Kate Fox, "The Kleenex for Men Crying Game Report: A Study of Men and Crying," Social Issues Research Centre, September

2004, http://www.sirc.org/publik/crying_game.pdf, 2. The numbers may have changed since, but presumably not very much.

2. For more on emotional health, check out Daniel Coleman's *Emotional Intelligence* (New York: Bantam Books, 2005).

3. Audrey Nelson, "The Crying Game," *Psychology Today,* January 2, 2011, http://www.psychologytoday.com/blog/he-speaks-she-speaks/201101/the-crying-game.

4. C. S. Lewis, *The Abolition of Man* (New York: HarperCollins, 2009), 24, 1.

5. David Brooks, "The Heart Grows Smarter," *New York Times,* November 5, 2012, http://www.nytimes.com/2012/11/06/opinion/brooks-the-heart-grows-smarter.html?_r=0.

6. Joshua Wolf Shenk, "What Makes Us Happy," *The Atlantic,* June 2009, http://www.theatlantic.com/magazine/archive/2009/06/what-makes-us-happy/307439/.

7. Ruki Sayid, "Tear We Go: Men Cry More at Footie than the Birth of their First Child," *Mirror,* June 7, 2012, http://www.mirror.co.uk/news/uk-news/men-cry-more-at-football-than-the-birth-864707.

Chapter 10: Find the Right Arena: The Fighting Man

1. Read the brilliant biography by Walter Isaacson, *Steve Jobs* (New York: Simon & Schuster, 2011).

2. In fact, men committing violence is a major problem. In the United States, men commit two-thirds of the violent crimes. (U.S. Department of Justice, "Criminal Victimization in the United States, 2007 Statistical Tables," Bureau of Justice Statistics, February 2010, http://bjs.ojp.usdoj.gov/content/pub/pdf/cvus0702.pdf, table 29). Johan Galtung, who founded the peace studies movement (and is himself a controversial figure) wrote, "To say that 95% of direct violence [in the world] is committed by men is probably an understatement." See Johan Galtung, *Peace by Peaceful Means* (London: Sage, 2006), 41.

3. Much of the following is developed from Nira Kfir's analysis of the four basic motivations and corresponding things we avoid. Kfir is part of the school of thought that began with Alfred Adler, the influential twentieth-century psychoanalyst. For a short overview, see Harold Mosak, *A Primer of Adlerian Psychology* (NewYork: Brunner-Routledge, 1999), 66–66. See also Kfir's recent work, *Personality and Priorities: A Typology* (Bloomington: Authorhouse, 2011).

Chapter 11: Get What You Want: The Heroic Man

1. Quentin Tarantino, *Kill Bill 2*, directed by Quentin Tarantino (Miramax, 2004).
2. Isaiah 53; 2 Corinthians 5:21.
3. For example, Luke 4:1.
4. John 5:19.
5. Luke 22:42.
6. Mark 1:35.
7. John 19:27.
8. John 15:15.
9. Hebrews 4:15.
10. Romans 3:23.
11. John 6:29.

Chapter 12: Living as the Forgiven Man

1. For more on how this works out, see my sermon on the Trinity at http://thejourney.org/media/doctrine/trinity-god.
2. Luther understood this as *simul justus et peccator*. We are simultaneously justified before God, but also sinners. That gives us the confidence to stare our sin in the face and confess it, as we know we have already been accepted by God. (Martin Luther, *Faith and Freedom: An Invitation to the Writings of Martin Luther*, eds. John F. Thornton and Susan B. Varenne (New York: Random House, 2002), xx.
3. The lyrics to the song are available here: http://www.lyricsdepot .com/harry-chapin/cats-in-the-cradle.html. Accessed April 16, 2013.

4. John Piper, *What Jesus Demands from the World* (Wheaton: Crossway, 2006), 126.
5. Tim Elmore, *Artificial Maturity: Helping Kids Meet the Challenge of Becoming Authentic Adults* (San Francisco: Jossey-Bass, 2012), 88.

ABOUT THE AUTHOR

DARRIN PATRICK SERVES AS THE chaplain of the St. Louis Cardinals. He founded the Journey in 2002, a church where dudes feel at home in St. Louis, Missouri. Darrin is vice president of the Acts 29 Church Planting Network. He has written two books, *Church Planter* and *For the City*, and has a doctorate degree from Covenant Seminary.

PHOTO COURTESY OF LISA HESSEL,
WWW.LISAHESSELPHOTOGRAPHY.COM

For Pastor Darrin's sermon and blog media content, speaking requests, book information, and more, visit: DarrinPatrick.org

———

Follow Pastor Darrin on Twitter:
@DarrinPatrick

Follow Pastor Darrin on Facebook:
Facebook.com/DarrinPatrick

———

For more information about the Journey, visit:
TheJourney.org